John Mooney, 34, has reported on crime and terrorism for newspapers and broadcasters for over ten years. He is the Crime Correspondent for the *Sunday Times*.

He wrote and devised *The Underworld*, a four part documentary series broadcast on *RTE* television in 2003. He also produced *Sabhair ach Salach*, a series profiling Ireland's richest criminals for *TG4* in 2006.

His first book, *Gangster* (2001), the biography of drugs trafficker John Gilligan, was a No. 1 bestseller.

His second book, *Black Operations: The Secret War Against the Real IRA* (2003), co-written with Michael O'Toole, is still considered the definitive account on the Real IRA and the 1998 Omagh bombing.

Rough Justice: Memoirs of a Gangster, (2004) which he ghost wrote for the Dublin criminal Maurice 'Bo Bo' Ward, was also a bestseller.

THE TORSO IN THE CANAL

THE INSIDE STORY ON IRELAND'S MOST GROTESQUE KILLING

THE TORSO IN THE CANAL

THE INSIDE STORY ON IRELAND'S MOST GROTESQUE KILLING

JOHN MOONEY

Every effort has been made to contact the copyright holders of material reproduced in this text. In cases where these efforts have been unsuccessful, the copyright holders are asked to contact the publishers directly.

Published by Maverick House, Main Street, Dunshaughlin, Co. Meath., Ireland.
Maverick House SE Asia, 440 Sukhumvit Road, Washington Square, Klongton, Klongtoey, Bangkok 10110, Thailand.

www.maverickhouse.com
email: info@maverickhouse.com

ISBN 978-1-905379-38-5

Copyright for text © 2007 John Mooney & Jean Harrington.
Copyright for typesetting, editing, layout, design
© Maverick House.

Printed and bound by ColourBooks Ltd.

5 4 3 2 1

The paper used in this book comes from wood pulp of managed forests. For every tree felled at least one tree is planted, thereby renewing natural resources.

A CIP catalogue record for this book is available from the British Library.

DEDICATION

For my parents.

ACKNOWLEDGEMENTS

This book is an account of the untimely killing and dismemberment of Farah Swaleh Noor, a Kenyan immigrant whose dismembered remains were found in the Royal Canal in north central Dublin, in March 2005.

The victim had been stabbed to death inside a flat at Richmond Cottages, where his body was then dismembered in a brutal fashion.

Various parts of his body were dumped in the canal, while his head was taken away and hidden in a public park, and then moved to another location, from where it vanished.

The killing gripped Ireland for obvious reasons. There was an initial suspicion that Noor was the victim of a ritual sacrifice.

When it emerged that two sisters from a working class estate in Dublin—Charlotte and Linda Mulhall—were behind the killing, I became interested in the story.

What follows is an account of the killing, or specifically the killers' recollections of the tragic events. It is worth noting that no one will ever know the full truth about what happened; all the statements gathered by the detectives tasked with establishing the truth contradict each other.

The two participants in the killing were drunk and had taken drugs on the night; therefore their recollections cannot be fully relied upon.

In the course of writing this book, I interviewed as many people as I could to establish what had happened. I also took information from documents prepared for the sisters' trials. In everyone I approached, I found a willingness to help. In this regard, I offer my eternal thanks to the detective team at Mountjoy, Fitzgibbon and Store Street Garda Stations, who were tasked with investigating Noor's killing. Their willingness to reveal the specifics about the case is not forgotten.

I would also like to express my sincere thanks to those who knew Charlotte and Linda Mulhall, and agreed to share their experiences with me. Members of the sisters' extended family, their neighbours, and some friends gave me an insight into the women's personalities, their social backgrounds and their family history. Some of this information has not been published to protect the privacy of various people.

I am also indebted to Noor's former partner, who revealed the intimate details of the time she spent with him. The harrowing accounts of the beatings and attacks she suffered at his hands could not have been easy to recall. I thank her profusely for assisting me in the research of this book.

A number of legal sources also provided an insight into the mechanics of the trial; their advice was much appreciated.

Much of what follows was taken from evidence gathered by gardaí and used by the Director of Public Prosecutions in the trial of Linda and Charlotte Mulhall heard before the Central Criminal Court. I have used information contained in the book of evidence to tell the story. I thank everyone who passed me these documents for their assistance.

On a personal note, I would like to thank my immediate friends, family and colleagues. Among them Fr Seamus Ahearne of Finglas; Todd O'Loughlin, Ian O'Reilly of the *BBC World Affairs Unit*; John Kealey, Des Gibson, Paul Sheridan and Michael O'Toole of *The Star*; Seán Curtain of *Press 22*, and my colleagues at the *Sunday Times*, particularly my editor Frank Fitzgibbon, John Burns and Liam Clarke.

There are others in An Garda Síochána, whom I consider friends but cannot individually name for confidentiality reasons, but their help, and above all friendship, is never forgotten and is much valued.

In this regard, I would also like to posthumously thank Kevin Stratford, an officer who tragically died last year after an all too short battle with cancer. Kevin was very much an inspiration to anyone who had ever met him; he is still sadly missed by his family, friends and colleagues. I was privileged to have known him.

Thanks are also due to the staff at Maverick House Publishers; Adam Hyland, Gert Ackermann, Sarah Ormston and Pornchai Sereemongkonpol; those at Gill Hess, who ensured the project ran smoothly, and Gerry Kelly at ColourBooks Ltd, for moving mountains.

I would also to thank Claire Foley at William Fry Solicitors for her help in preparing the manuscript for publication.

Finally I would like to thank Jean Harrington for her time and effort in helping to write, edit and work on the manuscript. Without her help, this book would never have been published.

John Mooney
January 2007

CHAPTER ONE

'Death is not the worst thing that can happen to men.'

- *Plato*

SHE WAS, SHE later remembered, always in the wrong place at the wrong time. Life had thrown her blow after blow; good luck and fortune had never visited her.

Linda Mulhall often said her life had been a downward spiral of depression and hopelessness for years. There is no doubt that this affected her life in every way. She had turned to drugs as a form of escapism when she was in her teens, and left school early. She went on to have four children, but the relationship broke down. Her next relationship had proved equally disastrous. Her partner physically abused her children. It was, she would later recall, the lowest point in her life.

Eventually this partner was charged and convicted; now she lived as a single mother. In many ways, she was an emotionally damaged woman. Those who know her say she craved love and contact. This revealed itself through little idiosyncrasies in her character; if she hugged someone, she would not let go. She would often embrace strangers in a very personal way, never breaking eye contact with them, and holding them tightly.

The only stabilising influence in her life was her four children, whom she loved, cared for and cherished, as best she could.

Linda, though, was not bitter; she quelled the monotony of life by drinking and taking drugs, including heroin. She rarely went out because she always had difficulty finding a babysitter. That's why the morning of 20 March 2005 was different.

On that morning, she was lounging around the house when her sister Charlotte asked if she would like to meet their mother Kathleen that afternoon. The two sisters were both staying in the family home in Kilclare Gardens, a sprawling housing estate in Fettercairn in Tallaght, the giant suburb that lies at the foothills of the Dublin Mountains.

Linda's first reaction was to say no to her little sister, who she fondly called Charlie. She was looking after her children and, in any event, she was too busy and too tired to go drinking. But Charlotte persisted: 'Come on, we'll have a laugh.'

Linda thought for a brief moment, before she asked if she could bring one of her sons along. She didn't expect Charlotte to understand why she wanted to take the boy, but she knew by the way she looked at her that this wasn't really an option. Charlotte wanted to have fun; that meant drinking.

At that moment, their father John came into the room. He was the breadwinner of the Mulhall family, which had seen more than its fair share of human agony. For a start, he had separated from his wife Kathleen after she left him for an African immigrant whom she met through Linda; his name was Farah Swaleh Noor. In the social context of life on a working class estate in Tallaght, the news that Kathleen had left him for an immigrant was crushing. It was something that few people could comprehend, least of all him. He had married Kathleen when they were in their teens but the relationship went nowhere from the start. He was deeply violent to his wife in the beginning. He had been a heavy drinker and watched films with strong scenes of violence.

Kathleen had remained at his side for years but fell for Noor soon after meeting him. She had initially moved her young boyfriend into the family home, forcing her husband to leave and move out for over a year, though he eventually returned when they moved to Cork. He had gotten on with his life as best he could.

Though he no longer cared for his wife, he had overheard the conversation and offered to mind Linda's children in order to give his daughter a rest. He probably thought she needed to unwind and relax. Linda didn't need any encouragement and thanked her father. The two sisters went upstairs to get ready.

Although it was early in the afternoon, they drank some vodka. They then left the house about an hour later and caught the No. 77 bus into Dublin city centre.

The streets were thronged with tourists and revellers who'd come to partake in the St Patrick's Day festivities, though it was far from a carnival atmosphere. There were people drinking everywhere, which gave an edge to the ambience.

When they stepped off the bus, Charlotte called her mother on her mobile phone. She could hear that Kathleen was in high spirits. She said she was wandering around with Noor on Upper O'Connell Street, and asked if they would walk towards them. The best place to meet, Kathleen suggested, was the McDonald's restaurant on Upper O'Connell Street.

The walk took Linda and Charlotte no more than five minutes. When they met their mother, they noticed she was holding hands with Noor. Linda interpreted this as a good omen. It was no secret that Noor often beat Kathleen and subjected her to extreme violence. Kathleen had told her daughters about the domestic abuse she suffered on more than one occasion.

As they embraced, Kathleen noticed Linda's upper lip was swollen from a piercing she had inserted. Linda was her favourite daughter, and always had been. She held Linda's face in her hands and examined the swelling.

Noor had said nothing until now. He too commented on the swollen tissue and blamed the swelling on the quality of the metal used in the piercing. He thought for a moment, then suggested they go to a shop where Linda could get a replacement piercing, something made from a superior metal. He pointed them in the direction of Lower O'Connell Street.

Noor stood out as he walked with the two sisters and their mother. He was a Kenyan immigrant, with an athletic build, but that wasn't what attracted attention; it was his girlfriend.

For a start, he was much younger and black; she was a white, middle-aged woman—visibly older than her boyfriend, though she still retained some youthfulness. The age difference between the two tended to draw unwanted glances from passers-by.

Most of the time Noor didn't notice strangers looking at him; much of his life was spent in a drunken stupor. And that day was no exception.

Noor led them straight to an off-licence in Dunnes Stores on Talbot Street, rather than the jewellers' shop he had mentioned. He rarely, if ever, drank in bars as he drank spirits by the litre. Instead he walked around the streets drinking from a bottle, or sometimes took beer back to his flat. On that afternoon, Noor wanted to drink vodka straight, so when he emerged from the shop, he slurped from the bottle. Kathleen and her daughters looked on, deciding what to do next.

None of them fancied drinking vodka straight, so Kathleen bought three bottles of Coke, which she handed out. They would use these as mixers to dilute the vodka. On any other day, they would have been stopped by gardaí and arrested for drinking in public, but the streets were full of people drinking beer. They blended in with the crowds.

Noor did eventually find the piercing shop, enabling Linda to buy a new lip piercing for €7. Holding her lip, she inserted this into her skin, which eased the pain a little. She then drank some more alcohol.

When they emerged from the shop, the streets were thronged, too thronged for what they planned to do next.

Linda was not a recreational drug user; she took drugs whenever possible to escape from the monotony of her life. She had brought some ecstasy tablets to help her unwind. She didn't want to risk taking the pills in public, so she wandered towards the boardwalk, which overlooks the River Liffey, as it runs through central Dublin.

The boardwalk was erected by the city authorities for the benefit of tourists and office workers, but it soon became a hangout for the city's homeless, drug addicts and winos. These intermingled with the tourists. As far as Linda was concerned, this made it an ideal place to drink and take some drugs.

As far as she was concerned, both she and Charlie were now having fun. Slightly drunk and a bit raucous, she slipped one of the tiny white tablets to Charlotte. She had brought about 10 with her—plenty for a good night.

Although Kathleen was slightly drunk, she noticed Linda passing the tablet to Charlotte, and asked what it was. Linda told her.

Why Kathleen didn't express horror at her daughter's decision to take drugs is unknown; on the contrary, ecstasy didn't seem to have criminal connotations for the middle-aged woman.

In such an environment anything went, so, according to Linda, Kathleen asked for one of the tiny white pills. This was the kind of behaviour that most women her age could never have dreamed about, but Linda duly obliged. Noor was the only one who declined the offer of a free pill. He said he wasn't in the mood.

Soon after they swallowed the pills, the sisters became giggly; they were loved up. The effects of the drug on Kathleen were not so obvious.

It was at this point that the atmosphere changed. Noor began to argue and bicker with Kathleen for no apparent reason. Linda couldn't help but overhear them rowing but she found it hard, almost impossible, to understand the Kenyan's accent. In fact, she had never really understood it since they first met. Noor spoke with a heavy accent, which she could not decipher no matter how hard she tried.

Anyway, she didn't want to listen to them argue; she was there to have a good time. Instead she listened to some music on her mobile phone. This was one of her many ways of switching off.

The atmosphere soon deteriorated. While the ecstasy made Linda and Charlotte feel more euphoric, Kathleen's mood turned sour. Moments later, she said she'd had enough, and decided it was time for them to move on.

It was now beginning to get dark, which prompted Linda to ask where they'd go next. There was only one place they could go, which was the flat that Kathleen shared with Noor. In truth they had no choice; none of the bars in central Dublin would have allowed them entry.

Kathleen and Noor continued to argue in raised voices as Linda walked away, followed by Charlotte, who came from behind and linked her arm. As they walked, Linda looked over her shoulder, and glanced behind.

'Are they still fighting?' she asked.

'Yeah.'

At this stage, Noor was now his usual drunken self; he was aggressive and argumentative towards Kathleen. He was looking for a row and began pushing his weight around. He was unable to walk in a straight line; instead he staggered and slurred his words.

While he made his way up O'Connell Street, he accosted a young Chinese boy. In his drunken state, he thought it was his son, a boy he fathered after forcing himself on a Chinese woman years earlier.

'Kathy, this is my son. This is my son,' he said, holding the terrified youngster by the shoulder. Kathleen looked down at the boy, who had burst into tears.

'That's not your son you bleeding eejit,' shouted Kathleen.

'It is my son. I know my own son.'

'It's not your fucking son.'

The boy was no more than five years old. He screamed in fright and cried out for help, shouting to his friends to come save him. They stood watching, too afraid to go near Noor.

Linda dragged him off, berating him for frightening the boy, momentarily causing Noor to release his grip. The boy ran away, screaming for help. Noor took no notice of this because he was so drunk he could barely speak.

Charlotte led the way to 17 Richmond Cottages; the flat Noor shared with their mother in the north inner city. The party had walked no more than a few metres when Noor then stumbled into Mohammed Ali Abu Bakaar and a woman named Deirdre Hyland.

Bakaar was a Somali, and had known Noor from the fishing port of Kismayu where the two had worked together. Noor had been one of thousands of immigrant fishermen who fished near the mouth of the Jubba River, on the Indian Ocean. Noor was a Bajuni; a race of mixed Bantu and Arab ancestry. He spoke Bajuni, which enabled him to work in the port. That he should meet a fisherman from Kismayu while drunk in Dublin during the St Patrick's weekend festivities was a one in a million chance encounter.

Noor recognised his friend, even though he was completely drunk and the words he used to greet him were slurred. Bakaar embraced him and greeted Kathleen, whom he called Katherine, before urging Noor to go home and sleep.

Bakaar would later call to mind that Kathleen took the brief opportunity to introduce her two daughters, Linda and Charlotte, to him. He was polite, and greeted them, before telling Noor to go home once more. He knew Noor of old. The remark must have annoyed Kathleen because she responded by saying: 'Just leave him alone, he's okay.'

The time was now 5.30pm. Although it was getting dark, Bakaar noticed how much Noor had changed since the time they first met on the fishing boats in Kismayu. He was particularly struck by

Noor's assimilation into Irish society; the fact that he was wearing an Irish soccer jersey with green and white stripes said it all.

*****

Noor and Kathleen continued to argue as they made their way back towards their flat. There was no stopping them. They continued to bicker until they arrived home at approximately 6.30pm that evening. It was now cold and dark.

The flat they rented was located in a two storey house divided into four apartments. It was on the ground floor to the front of the house. They hadn't been there long having just moved back to Dublin from Cork.

The vodka and ecstasy had turned what had started as a minor row into a bitter argument; the two continued to row without pausing as they walked through the front door. Linda and Charlotte ignored them; they were having a good time, and that was all that mattered. In this regard, Charlotte put on a Sean Paul CD she had given to Noor as a gift, and then sat on the couch.

She was more familiar with the living arrangements than Linda, who had never visited before.

The ecstasy in their bloodstreams had now taken full effect. Linda drifted along, not really thinking of anything in particular. She was a regular drug user so the ecstasy didn't affect her like it did Charlotte. Linda's body was somewhat immune to amphetamines.

At this moment, Kathleen presented Noor with a glass of lager poured from a can. The drink was a turning point in the day. According to evidence later given in court, Kathleen had spiked the alcohol with an ecstasy tablet she had crushed. Noor didn't suspect a thing and took the glass of beer without any hesitation and began to drink.

Linda later explained in a statement produced in evidence that she suspected Kathleen gave Noor the tablet so that he would share the good feelings her daughters were experiencing:

'I think Ma wanted Farah to have the E as me and Charlie were in great humour,' she said.

Charlotte's statement to gardaí shows that she was of the same view. However, she said that she took more ecstasy after arriving in the flat.

'That's when me ma put one in Farah's drink so that he would be on the same buzz as us. Then me ma starts arguing, I don't know what they started arguing about,' she said later.

Despite the relative potency of the drug, the only effect it had on Noor was to increase his sexual appetite. The drug didn't cause him to feel closer to his girlfriend, or even become a little restless. All he felt was an attraction for Linda. Little by little, as the minutes passed, he began taking more notice of her.

All three women knew Noor was a predatory male in almost every sense of the word. He had physically and sexually abused women all his life; he looked on them as objects rather than people with individual personalities. He sometimes flirted with them, sometimes raped them, and sometimes beat them. He once boasted about killing one.

Whether it was the ecstasy he unwittingly consumed or his own desires, his interest in Linda became more apparent as the hours passed. Charlotte sensed it, perhaps more than anyone present in the room. The constant attention and looks he directed at Linda were tolerable for a time but worsened as he got more drunk, and the ecstasy pill took effect.

It was at this point that he set in train a series of events that would end his life.

There were few places to sit in flat No. 1: this caused Linda to sit on Charlotte's lap as she sat beside Noor on a sofa.

'Me and Charlie were having a laugh. I was sitting on Charlie's lap on the red settee. Farah was sitting beside me and Ma was on the arm,' Linda would later recollect.

Noor, who was flirtatious, saw the opportunity to get closer to Linda. Whilst sitting on the couch, he pulled Linda close to him, and then placed his arms around her waist. She was drunk, but sober enough to know what was happening; more importantly that he was her mother's boyfriend. She tried to pull away without causing a scene but Noor wouldn't let go; his grip was too tight. She later recalled:

'It did not feel right. He pulled me closer to him, sort of touching on Charlie's lap and his knee. His arm went from my back onto my shoulder and he pulled me close to him. He said something in my ear.

'I did not understand him but I knew it was dirty. It was something he should not have said to me. It caused me to shiver.'

Linda did not shout at Noor, though Charlotte saw what was happening. Rather than stay silent, she told him to get his hands off her sister. Noor was now so drunk and stoned that he wasn't even listening, nor did he care what she said. He took no notice of the warning and continued as if she had said nothing. He was fumbling about.

Noor then pulled Linda closer, moved in closer to her and whispered into her ear once more. This time, he called her a creature of the night, and then said she was like her mother.

This was a catalyst for trouble. Linda then spoke.

'I said "Farah get your hands off me." He whispered something in my ear like, "You and me are creatures of the night." I did not know what he meant. It was something he used to say to me ma.'

According to Linda's account of what happened that night, she then asked her mother what he meant. Noor was still holding her waist, though occasionally his hand would touch her leg. That he wouldn't let go further exacerbated the situation.

Noor had never touched Linda before, although she knew he had violent tendencies towards women; he had left her mother hospitalised in the past.

'He still had a grip of me and me ma said, "What do you mean? What do you mean by saying to Linda that we are two creatures of the night?"'

If Linda had reacted to Noor's unwanted advances in a muted manner, there was no disguising the anger that Charlotte felt towards him. She became hysterical. She began screaming and shouting.

'What the fuck are you doing?'

Whether Noor was just drunk or simply too high on ecstasy to understand the seriousness of the situation, he failed to release his hold of Linda, who had now struggled to her feet. He held his grip to annoy the women, as much as anything else.

'I was trying to say "Get your hands off of me," but his hands were still around my waist. I really don't think he could see me ma and Charlotte. I was now standing beside the sink and Farah was standing in front of me.

'I was trying to push Farah's hands from my waist. I said to me ma as I tried to push his hands away, "He would sleep with your daughter as quick as he would look at you."'

It was at this point that Charlotte also stood up and told Noor to stop. She had purpose in her voice and her body language was threatening. But he didn't stop. Instead he taunted her, continuing to say: 'You're so like your mammy.'

In a statement she made to detectives, Linda maintains to this day that Charlotte attacked Noor while trying to protect her. There is no doubt that Noor refused to release his grip because he was being asked to; he wasn't going to allow himself to be bossed around by women.

'Charlotte was saying, "Get your hands off her. She is nothing like me ma. Get your hands off Linda." Charlie was stronger and was putting it up to Farah saying, "Get your hands away from her."'

Still the warning had no effect.

'Farah would still not get his hands off me.'

The tension in the room was palpable. Noor pushed Kathleen away with one hand, and drew his finger across his throat in a threatening manner. He insinuated he would kill someone.

'Me ma pushed Farah, pushed him back towards the bedroom,' Linda later stated.

It could be surmised that Noor was fooling around and meant no harm. But he had a history of sexual violence towards women, and had beaten Kathleen, on one occasion breaking her ribs. This gave way to underlying tensions which had by this time spiralled out of control.

But Linda and Charlotte were suspicious of Noor for other reasons. They had been deeply affected when their mother had left the family for him. It was something they could not fathom; and now Charlotte was confronted by that same man threatening her sister.

*****

In the flat, on the kitchen draining board was an orange coloured Stanley blade that had been used to cut carpet. Charlotte could see the blade was sharp.

While Noor was looking at Kathleen, and still refusing to let Linda go, Charlotte reached for the blade and once again warned Noor to let her sister go. He took no notice of her. She then picked up the blade and stabbed him in the throat, inflicting what must have been a wound across his throat.

The wound may not have killed him but it did catch him by surprise. It was the beginning of a frenzied attack.

Noor stood up. Shock now engulfed his body as the blade penetrated an artery, causing him to lose consciousness. In her statement, Linda said he didn't fall down at once, but 'sort of staggered.'

Charlotte, in her interviews, which were later read out in court, claimed her mother handed the sisters the implements to kill Noor.

'Me ma just kept saying to me and Linda "Please kill him or he is going to kill me." She just kept going on about it. Me ma gave me a knife and she gave Linda a hammer. I don't know where she got them. I cut him on the neck on the side. I was facing him,' she said.

He stumbled backwards, his body probably reeling from the pain and sudden loss of blood to his brain. He could barely speak but managed to say the word 'Katie', which was his pet name for his girlfriend, Kathleen. He then fell back into a bedroom and hit his head on a bunk bed before collapsing to the ground.

It was at this stage that Linda began attacking him with a hammer.

According to her version of the events, she struck several blows to his head.

'I picked up a hammer from the sink and hit him on the head, loads of times; a good few times. He fell on to the ground and I hit him again. Charlie stabbed him,' she confessed.

The two women continued to attack Noor without any hesitation, or consideration given to the fact that he was now lying on the ground, and presented no threat to anyone. The amphetamines in their bloodstreams may well have induced manic psychosis, where each action worsened their mental condition and possibly resulted in more violence, and extreme abnormal behaviour. Whatever the cause; it was an orgy of grotesque violence they both engaged in.

Charlotte would later confess: 'I cut his neck. Linda hit him with the hammer, this was in the bedroom. I can't remember everything. I stabbed him in the neck. I don't remember how he died in the bedroom but he was dead.'

Charlotte had stabbed him in the upper torso and in the back, sinking another knife—a bread knife—in so deep in one attack that it punctured both of his lungs, ripped through his kidneys and perforated his liver. She didn't stop there.

Stab wounds can be made with minimal force. The important factor is the sharpness of the tip of the blade—once it has penetrated clothing and skin, remarkably little force is required to follow through and create a deep wound. In addition, the faster the stabbing action, the easier it is to penetrate skin.

Charlotte repeatedly stabbed her victim with as much strength as she could muster, inflicting fatal wounds right across his body, particularly his torso.

The first wound to his chest would have been enough to kill him, but high on ecstasy, Charlotte continued to plunge the knife into his lungs as he lay on the floor fighting to breathe. In truth, Noor never stood a chance. He was drunk and probably lost consciousness when he was struck by Linda, who also inflicted a series of blows which probably crushed his skull.

The blows would have resulted in a decreased amount of blood flow to the brain, depriving it of oxygen.

Noor's nervous system would also have decreased the amount of blood flow to the brain, as a protective mechanism, forcing him to pass out. This would have ensured he didn't fight back.

When they had finished, Noor lay on the floor covered in stab wounds, bloody and badly bruised. Linda had struck him with such ferocity that hammer marks were left in the floor.

No one knows for sure what emotions ran through their minds at that moment in time, or what it was that led them to engage in a final act of barbarism. It may have been drug induced hypomania. The chances are it was.

The most accurate account of what happened is contained in Linda's statement in which she gave the following version of events.

'Charlie said, "Is he alive; is he alive? I thought he was coming at me." Farah was lying on the ground and Charlie said to me ma that he was dead. Me ma said, "Get him out, get him out." We were all screaming at this stage.'

Terrified and gripped by panic, the two sisters dragged the body into the flat's bathroom where they stood over it. Charlotte's statement, read out during the course of the trial, implied that it was her mother who decided it would be best to dismember Noor, although she didn't use those words.

However, Linda's statement contradicts this and quotes Charlotte as saying: 'We will chop him up.'

It was never determined who came up with the idea but whatever happened, the two began to denigrate their victim's body through dismemberment.

CHAPTER TWO

'To profane a dead body by cutting it to pieces has always seemed, at least to our Western eyes, an act of bestial brutality. It is one thing to do murder. It is quite another to destroy the murder victim's identity, and this is the effect of dismemberment.'

- *Dr William R. Maples, forensic anthropologist, in* Dead Men Do Tell Tales

THERE ARE NUMEROUS ways of hiding a body and erasing proof of a murder. Those most frequently used are burial of the victim's body at a secret location such as a remote wood, mountain, or a construction site. Sometimes killers burn the bodies of their victims using accelerants, until all traces of the crime have been erased and identification of the victim is almost impossible.

Other killers have been known to drop a weighted-down body in the open sea or in a lake in the hope that it will never be found. Dismemberment is, by far, the rarest method of body disposal. Few killers have the stomach or nerve to take an axe, or a saw, to a body and begin cutting it into small pieces.

Women are rarely accused of denigrating a victim's body in such fashion. Of the handful of cases of those who do, dismemberment is almost always carried out immediately after the crime, usually in a blind panic.

Perhaps they went into shock when they realised the gravity of what they had done; in many ways this would have given them a very limited ability to understand their actions, while helping them to suspend reality while they went about their gruesome task. Neither of the two appear to have planned what took place; instead the events just unfolded. When they realised that no one could help them, they got on with the task of dismembering Noor's body.

*****

The actual dismemberment took place in the bathroom of the flat. This was small and pokey. Therefore, when the sisters dragged Noor's body into the bathroom, they found there was no room to move; certainly not enough to dismember a corpse.

At this point, Charlotte sat on the toilet seat while Linda positioned herself in the shower. This gave them some room to manoeuvre.

According to the statements given by both Charlotte and Linda, Kathleen did not participate in the dismemberment. Instead, she sat in the kitchen smoking continuously.

The tools they used to dissect the body were the same implements they had used to kill Noor— a Stanley knife and a hammer, and the bread knife that had perforated his vital organs.

Charlotte was the one who began the vile process of dismemberment when she attempted to saw through one of Noor's arms with the bread knife.

Her statement read: 'We got Farah into the bathroom. Myself and Charlie dragged him in by the legs, and me and Charlie cut him up. It was Charlie's idea. Charlie started sawing on his arms, with the knife; the knife had a rugged edge on it.

'She cut into his arms with the knife, she got tired. I then used the hammer and hit his legs a number of times. It took us a few hours to do it. Me and Charlie took turns cutting him and breaking the bones.'

The Stanley knife made an unsuitable tool for dismemberment. While the same knife had cut Noor's flesh with relative ease, it was unable to divide the cartilage and bone without excessive effort. However, this resistance didn't stop Charlotte, who had boundless energy from the ecstasy in her bloodstream. It should be remembered the two of them had taken more ecstasy tablets.

Although the sawing action was exhausting, Charlotte cut and cut at the body with the knife until she could cut no more. Linda sat beside her, helping and encouraging her. When they encountered resistance in the form of bone and cartilage, Charlotte didn't give up. Instead she took hold of the hammer and began to strike Noor's legs in a battering fashion. While this motion was aimed at dismembering his joints, it caused the body to haemorrhage excessive amounts of blood, which spilled from the body.

A man of Noor's size and weight normally has about 5.6 litres of blood—Charlotte's butchery caused much of this to depart from the body. This flowed on to the floor. In a desperate attempt to stem this, the two women placed towels around the severed wounds, but this had little effect. The blood continued to flow; there was nothing they could do to stop it.

The bathroom of the flat now resembled a slaughter house; a horrid smell engulfed the room and permeated everywhere. It was foul. Of the night in question, Linda would later say the 'smell was ... it wouldn't go away. I think about it every night.'

The act of dismemberment proved to be a highly physical process for the sisters. Charlotte continued to tear and hammer at the bones and sinews that somehow held Noor's legs together.

Sweat poured from her body, and her arms were soon covered in blood and pieces of flesh. The scene was one from the bowels of hell; nothing had prepared them for this. They tried looking away from the body but it was no use. They also changed positions and swapped implements on several occasions but it didn't make the butchering process any faster. When one got tired of hammering, they would rest by using a knife to cut at another section of the body.

One noticeable fact was that they used no coherent method to dismember Noor's remains. High on drugs, confused and terrified, they just cut away and hammered at the victim's flesh and bones, mutilating him, in no methodical way.

Perhaps the most gruesome part of the dismemberment was Linda's decision to remove the victim's penis. This was a brutal act of barbarism.

'Me ma had told me already that he had raped her and I said, "He won't rape me Ma again." I cut his private parts off, the long piece, not the balls,' she later said.

The mutilation of the genitalia was significant insofar as it had nothing to do with disposing of the body but everything to do with revenge. Noor had beaten and attacked women; by cutting off his penis, Linda believed she was avenging the violence he had dispensed on her mother.

In total, the sisters spent five hours cutting Noor's corpse into eight separate pieces of varying weights and sizes.

The largest body segment was the upper torso, which involved his disembowelment, revealing his intestines and internal organs.

Once this bloody act had been accomplished, his lower torso was left with the hip joints fully intact; it should be noted that they had earlier cut off his legs, but now they removed the femurs, leaving his lower legs intact with the feet attached.

His right and left upper limbs were also broken above the humerus using the claw hammer; this was difficult as a variety of muscles were attached. When he had been alive, these enabled movement at the elbow and at the shoulder. Now they held what remained of his body together. These particular muscles were hard to cut through as Noor had been strong and athletic in life.

The head was the final body part to be removed.

In their subsequent statements to gardaí, both sisters admitted that they took turns at cutting it from the torso.

However, removing the head was particularly traumatic for Linda, who later recalled that she wasn't able to look at the face while she cut and hammered.

She was consumed by guilt, which she somehow managed to block from her mind. In many ways, she was unable to evaluate the situation she found herself in. Rather than even think about what she and Charlotte were doing, even for a second, she forged ahead with the cutting.

Of course, they knew the life had long since gone from Noor's eyes, but they still haunted Linda. She could not help but look at the expression on his face while she engaged in the savagery.

The look of terror was too much. Eventually, she placed a towel over his face while she finished hammering his neck, in a final attempt to dislocate it from the shoulders. This made it easier for her to butcher the body and cut off the head.

It was a bloody operation, as the towels were completely ineffective at soaking up the blood that flowed from every wound. In fact there was so much blood that a crimson pool formed on the floor.

'I had the towel over his head, over his face, and kept using the hammer. It would not come off. Both of us had to take turns with the hammer. I did not think about chopping it up but Charlotte said to do it,' she said in a statement.

Linda and Charlotte were now completely panic-stricken and called their father. Linda rang John Mulhall Snr from her mobile at 11.41pm as Noor lay dead on the floor. They spoke for about two minutes and Linda told him what had happened. It is likely that he couldn't understand his daughter or didn't believe her, as he rang his estranged wife ten minutes later to verify if what Linda had said was true—if they had actually killed Farah Swaleh Noor. He also spoke to Kathleen for about two minutes, before speaking to her briefly one last time just before midnight. All three women had consumed drink and several ecstasy tablets, so perhaps it took him some time to comprehend what had happened.

*****

Now they had finished butchering him, it was time to dispose of the body. This would be the most important part of the killing. The dismemberment had already taken six to seven hours. It was now night and the streets around Richmond Cottages and the north inner city were largely empty apart from the odd vagrant wandering around.

Their father had initially thought that Linda and Charlotte were high on drugs when they called to say what they'd done. Though, when he thought about the conversation, he began to panic. While he wanted to believe his daughters were claiming to have killed Noor because they were high; something in their voices caused him to worry. Driven by fear, more than anything else, he drove from his home into the city. He arrived there at 1.30am.

He rang the flat's doorbell and walked in. When he walked through the front door, he saw Linda, Charlotte and his estranged wife. The flat was clean, almost as if nothing had happened. Neither Linda nor Charlotte was soiled by blood stains. He momentarily relaxed. He had been estranged from his wife for years but very much cared about his daughters.

According to the statement he later gave to detectives, he asked where Noor was. Linda told him his body was in the bedroom. He looked in the room but could see nothing. He returned momentarily, and said he wasn't there. He never suspected that the body had been dismembered.

Linda told him to look again, and then confessed as to what had happened—that they had dismembered his remains. He looked once again. This time he saw a black bin liner in the corner. It was full. He suddenly felt nauseous. He moved a little closer and momentarily glanced into the bag. What he saw made him run from the flat. He threw up on the steps. When he pulled himself together, he said he wanted to have nothing to do with them. He then left. He didn't care what happened to them. As far as he was concerned, they were on their own.

The departure of their father from the scene sent the women into a blind panic that gripped them, according to statements they later made. Though it should be noted that they made sure not to mention his visit to the flat in any of their subsequent interviews. It is also noteworthy that Kathleen also never mentioned her estranged husband's visit.

The effects of the alcohol and ecstasy were also beginning to wear off, making it more difficult for them to function as they were confronted by the reality of what they had done. However, their actions from this point onwards, suggest they still operated with some degree of clarity and forethought.

Realising they would have to act alone, they were careful not to try move the entire body at once. They had packed the separate body parts into black plastic bags; these were then placed into sports bags, Linda recalled:

'Charlotte started pulling the heavy pieces into sports bags. Charlotte put the main parts of the body into the sports bag; she put it into a black plastic bag at first. I put the legs into the black plastic bags but I let the legs come out.'

They then lifted the battered and bruised head into a plastic bag, which they placed in a suitcase. Rather than dispose of the head with the rest of the torso, they left it in the back garden of No. 17 while they went about disposing of the remaining body parts, one by one.

Linda would later admit it was her idea to separate the head from the body.

'I decided we were not throwing the head in. I said it to Charlotte so that it would not be identified.'

They all hoped the decision to hide the head elsewhere would ensure the gardaí would not identify the remains.

Perhaps their greatest mistake was to dump the body parts locally rather than at some remote location, away from the city. If the body parts had been hidden at several different locations, without leaving any clothing behind, it is likely the killing would have gone unnoticed, or certainly unsolved. But this was out of the question because neither Linda nor Charlotte drove a car. They couldn't transport the body out of the city so, due to the circumstances, they had no choice but to dispose of it locally.

While they figured it was the safest thing to do—moving the body parts through the city during daylight hours being too risky—it was also the clumsiest.

They carried the body parts to the Royal Canal, which flowed through the north inner city. It was no more than a five minute walk from Richmond Cottages.

The place they chose to dump the body was Clarke's Bridge, near Ballybough, just minutes away from the flat. In the dead of night, the two sisters carried the bags to the canal bank. Linda carried the light bits while Charlotte carried the heavier ones.

During the course of the trial, Linda's statement was produced as evidence. It indicated that her mother accompanied Charlotte and her when they went to move the bags, saying: 'Charlotte took the heavy bits, we walked down to the canal, me ma walked with us.'

As they made their way down the bank and under the bridge, they operated under the cover of darkness. When they stumbled down the bank, they opened a bag and threw a body part into the water.

They made the journey several times, all the time watching for passers-by or unwanted strangers. They could just about see what they were doing, it was so dark. After they had dumped the final body part; there was some panic about whether a scar on Noor's arm would identify him. Suddenly the sisters were gripped by fear, but by this stage, it was too late.

The torso, femurs, legs and arms had all sunk in the water. There was nothing more they could do, even if they wanted to.

*****

When they returned to the flat, they found the bathroom and bedroom covered in blood and tiny pieces of flesh. The violent manner in which Noor had died had left tell tale marks everywhere. His blood had soaked into carpets, linoleum and the wooden skirting boards around the flat. The scene was one of horror, with all the tell tale signs of death there to see.

Linda would afterwards confirm to gardaí that the carpet close to the bunk bed was heavily soiled with blood: 'There was more blood there than anywhere else.'

The towels they used to mop up the blood had also left crimson stains on the floor.

The sisters next set about washing these stains away using buckets, mops and clothes. The clean up lasted well into the night. Charlotte recalled that they stayed up all night.

'We were just cleaning up for hours. We had everything in the flat cleaned up then we went up to the Watergate Park and buried the head,' she later said.

As her statement indicates, the next stage of the cover up involved the disposal of Noor's head. It was crucial that it would never be found. Others would not have been so brazen to attempt it, but the decision to dispose of the head at another location was made while they were still partly drunk and high on drugs. This explains their bizarre decision to place the head in a bag, take it through the city centre, then carry it on a public bus, and to a place where it could be disposed of safely. In many ways, the audacity of this would help ensure its success.

They stayed up all night long cleaning away all traces of blood before they left Richmond Cottages the next morning. The time was now 11am. They were suffering from a mixture of shock, exhaustion and guilt; they were also hungry.

But they knew that to conceal their act, they had to dispose of the head as quickly as possible.

Having placed the head in a bag the night before, they now took it with them as they walked into a supermarket on Summerhill Parade to buy salad rolls, which they ate on the street. They were actually filmed in the store by an internal CCTV camera.

When they finished eating, they made their way into the city centre and caught a bus to The Square Shopping Centre in Tallaght. They paid the correct fares and didn't draw any unwanted attention to themselves.

With Noor's head still safely in the bag, they walked around the shopping centre, looking in the windows of clothes shops. They were now nursing headaches, but their minds and senses were also in turmoil.

Linda began to have flashbacks; she could not stop thinking about Noor, the look on his face when he died, and how he'd called out her mother's name after Charlotte had slashed his throat.

Inside, she felt she was trapped in a living nightmare. She possessed a magnified view of the death she could not escape from. The memory of the dismemberment made her sick. She had cut, torn, pulled and wrenched the body apart; removing his limbs and head. She had mutilated his body.

In truth, she was horrified by what she had done. She felt waves of nervousness, anxiety, hyperactivity and irritability. She couldn't hide her agitation, no matter how hard she tried. She also looked terrible.

Charlotte's mind was also in turmoil, though she managed to remain calm. She too was in the throes of a deep depression, terrified about what to do next. The reality of the situation the sisters found themselves in ignited a sense of paranoia. They now felt sick.

It is clear that they were in a state of denial. Admitting to themselves that they had killed Noor was hard enough, but admitting to dismemberment was something else. In many ways, strolling through the shopping centre was their means of normalising the situation.

When they left the Square, they walked to the Sean Walsh Memorial Park in Tallaght. It was here they planned to bury Noor's head in the ground in the hope it would never be found.

The mentality shared by the two sisters was a confused one. In truth, they didn't know what to do or how to handle the situation. They certainly weren't thinking rationally; for a start they couldn't decide exactly where to conceal the head. Linda later recalled:

'Charlotte knows the park and we were saying "We will put it here and put it there." We walked around for ages. We sat down on a rock. We were looking for different places, where the bench was. Charlie started digging holes with the knife. The hole was not very deep. I had the head on me back and I said to Charlie, "Get this off me." Charlie took it out of the bag and put it in the hole. The head was still in the black bag. Charlie filled the hole. I could not do it.'

The hole she had dug lay a few feet away from a park bench. In a statement later produced in court, Linda said that their mother, who had accompanied them, 'took the knives and hammer and flung them into one of the park's lakes.'

'We then went home. I burned the bag in a fire at home in the sitting room. Me da was in bed.'

Although they convinced themselves that they had gotten away with the killing, the death continued to haunt them in the hours that followed.

Linda feared the body parts would be found in the canal. In fact, she was certain that someone would see something out of the ordinary, and find a body part. Her senses told her it was just a matter of time.

While Charlotte had the outward appearance of someone with not a care in the world, inside she too was beginning to break down. At one point, just days after the killing, she broke down and confessed to her sister Marie, who thought she was making up stories.

It was 6.30pm and Marie was just home from her job as an apprentice mechanic. She found Charlotte drunk when she walked into the house. She sat down beside her and comforted her, before Charlotte eventually said, 'We're after killing Farah Noor.'

Marie knew from previous experience that Charlotte was capable of telling wild stories, particularly when she was drunk. Marie kept quiet and just let Charlotte ramble on, thinking nothing more of the story. This time, Charlotte told a different version of the events that had taken place; she said that she had gone to the chipper with her mother, and when they returned, they found Noor trying to rape Linda.

Charlotte said she had first hit Noor, then Linda had hit him, causing him to fall. Marie would later make a statement which said: 'She did not describe the items used to hit Farah, nor did I enquire. Charlotte told me that they then cut Farah Noor into two halves and buried him either side of the canal. She did not identify the canal, nor did I ask her. I honestly did not believe her. Charlotte was very upset at this stage and I was shocked to put it mildly, by the story she told me even though I did not believe her.'

Marie, who was a rock of sense, thought nothing more of the story. She did not believe her younger sister and didn't press her for further details, as she thought that Charlotte was rambling.

Instead she went for a drive and when she returned, Charlotte had calmed down and was sitting on the couch, talking to their father. She appeared to be talking about normal matters, so Marie went to bed and didn't think anything more of the story. She didn't discuss it with anyone. However, it would later emerge that Marie played a significant role in getting her sister to speak to gardaí, once she realised there was truth in the story.

Perhaps, like Linda, Charlotte knew it was only a matter of time before the torso, or some other body part, was found in the water. As it would emerge, they were both right.

*****

Just hours after Charlotte and Linda had dumped the body parts into the canal, the torso began to float to the surface. It soon drew attention from passers-by who thought it looked like a body without a head. It floated because Noor's lungs were full of air.

The location where they dumped the other body parts, including the arms and legs, almost guaranteed they would be found. The section of canal under the bridge was the clearest, allowing anyone who happened to walk by a full view of the submerged body parts, though the women had no way of knowing this as they had dumped the body in the dead of night.

Margaret Gannon was one of the many people who saw the mutilated torso drifting in the dark waters on 21 March, a Monday. In her statement, she said she saw a black plastic bag wrapped in brown tape floating in the water. She didn't take much notice of it, but when she saw it again on Tuesday, she thought the bag looked like it contained a body with no head. She was struck by the sight but didn't believe her eyes, and continued about her business.

Three days later, Paul Kearney was cycling along the canal from Jones Road to Ballybough. He saw an arm and other body parts submerged in the water under Clarke's Bridge, known locally as Ballybough Bridge, but concluded that they were parts of a broken mannequin. He too didn't think for a moment that the body parts could be real.

On the evening of 30 March, Peter Steinle was walking beside the canal from North Strand Road, when he saw a number of body parts—this time they were floating in the water. He noticed an arm and hand, a second arm floating separately, two lower legs and feet with socks.

He was horrified by what he saw and rang Crimestoppers when he reached home. He left a message on the answering machine, saying he thought he saw body parts floating in the water.

The second person to alert the emergency services to the remains that day was one James O'Connor. He often walked along the banks of the Royal Canal. Around 6.30pm, some hours after Steinle had phoned Crimestoppers, O'Connor noticed a number of youths standing around the water at Clarke's Bridge. They told him without fear of contradiction there was a dummy in the water. Out of curiosity, he looked more closely; he thought he saw body parts but he wasn't sure.

For some reason, O'Connor felt that something was wrong but he wasn't sure what he was looking at. He could just about make out the shapes of the various body parts submerged in the water. Then, when he strained his eyes to look more closely, he began to see more body parts.

As his eyes wandered, he made out an arm, then a leg with a sock on the foot. As his eyes became accustomed to the dark water, he next saw what he thought was a torso and then a thigh. He immediately dialled 999 and asked for help.

His call was logged at 6.56pm at Tara Street Fire Station, a command and control centre in Dublin city. Fire officer Glen Mannelly took his call, which stated that there was a body in the Royal Canal.

The fire service presumed someone had fallen into the water, and dispatched two fire engines from the North Strand to retrieve the body. An emergency tender was sent at speed from Phibsboro while an ambulance rushed to the scene from Tara Street. Meanwhile, Garda Control was notified.

O'Connor waited on the canal bank for about five minutes when help arrived at 7.02pm. Derek Carroll was the district fire officer and the first to arrive at the scene. He spoke to O'Connor, who thanked him for coming and pointed in the direction where the body parts lay submerged in the water under the bridge.

Carroll looked into the water. He too could see a leg with a sock, the arm and other body parts. They looked real to him but like everyone else, there was a residual fear that this was an elaborate hoax. That's why Carroll instructed one of his fire crew, Andrew Cullen, to examine the body parts more closely.

It should be noted that the body parts had turned a marbled white colour as they decomposed in the canal water. This caused them to look somewhat artificial. This, more than anything, ensured that no one was quite sure what to make of the discovery. There was only one thing they could do.

Cullen retrieved a drag from the fire tender and plunged it into the water. This was a fork-like object used for searching ponds and rivers. It immediately caught one of the arms that had been resting in about seven feet of water directly under the bridge.

Those present watched the drag emerge from the water wondering whether or not they might be the victims of a hoax. However, once the arm emerged from the water, all those present knew it was real.

The fire crew knew by looking at the marbling of the skin tissue, coupled with the odour of rotting

flesh, that they had fou
fact, the body had decomp
because it had been dismem
body which have sustained tra
more rapidly than those that have n

The decomposing flesh smelt put
rotting and began to fall apart. There
mistaking its authenticity.

Cullen returned the arm to the water in order
preserve it. The fire crew then set about cordoning
off the scene in accordance with established
procedure. This was no longer their business; it
was a murder scene.

Garda Alan Greally had been on duty that
evening in Garda Command and Control. He had
been notified by Dublin Fire Brigade just after
7pm that there might be a body in the water at
Clarke's Bridge in the north inner city. He entered
the information gleaned from the emergency call
into the Garda's computer system, PULSE, as
Incident No. 050890972.

The report was initially communicated to
Fitzgibbon Street, the garda station nearest the
scene. When they received the news, nine officers
were sent to the canal within minutes, to seal off
the area. The call also went out to the station's
Detective Unit to make their way to the scene.

ded but
e dealing
not fully
mined to

ey began
e officer
stic bag
ds away

looked
ᵧ ....ing the
torso to float off. The bag was quickly retrieved and the area where it was found was marked with plastic markers.

It is standard procedure in cases where bodies are found in such circumstances to call a doctor. It may seem strange but the police at the scene were obliged to call a medic to pronounce death officially.

The doctor in question was Y.M. Fakih. He was met at the scene by Detective Sergeant Gerry McDonnell, one of the most experienced officers attached to the District Detective Unit at Fitzgibbon Street, who had arrived at the canal. He too saw what appeared to him to be mutilated limbs of a body submerged in the canal water.

There was obviously nothing the doctor could do but confirm the remains were human.

The body parts could not be moved that evening so they were left in the water overnight to preserve them and any evidence that may have been left behind. Uniformed gardaí were left guarding the canal bank to keep the public from contaminating the scene. By this time, news of the gruesome discovery had broken on the news bulletins. Photographers and journalists descended on the north inner city while curious onlookers gathered on the canal bridge.

Rumours of the torso in the canal spread among the residents of the local flat complexes and housing estates. Teenagers and curious onlookers gathered to watch: among them were Charlotte and Linda.

They had been watching the evening news when their worst fears were realised. Inside the flat, Linda cried uncontrollably when a report on the body find was broadcast. She could barely comprehend what was happening.

'We were all in the house crying. We then went down close to the bridge, close to where the guards had the tape. We walked on the side away from the Gala. We asked some people what was after happening. We went home and watched the news,' she later recalled.

A sense of blind panic consumed the sisters. Linda was unable to stop crying; Charlotte was also overrun by emotion. They comforted each other, and drank as much alcohol as possible in a desperate attempt to come to terms with what they had done, but also to quell a sense of terror that had quickly enveloped them.

Linda feared jail more than anything else. She thought about being separated from her children.

Charlotte was also gripped by fear. In fact, neither of them could eat properly nor sleep; instead they spent their waking hours trying to imagine what would happen.

*****

Meanwhile the ten days that had passed since they had killed Noor now seemed like an eternity. Linda, perhaps, more than Charlotte, knew things would never be the same again. No matter what way she examined the situation, no matter how much she tried to deny she would be caught, she could not escape from the fact that sooner or later, she knew someone was going to come looking for her. Waiting for this event to happen, more than anything else, terrified her.

The next time her sister Marie gave Charlotte's story more thought was when she heard that the body of a man had been found in the Royal Canal. She was sitting watching the news on *TV3* with her father when she saw the report. The location of the body meant nothing to her as she wasn't aware of where her mother lived, as she had dropped contact with her soon after Kathleen started going out with Noor. She had a brief conversation with her father about the news item, but did not discuss what Charlotte had drunkenly spoken about a few days previously. She would never have imagined that Charlotte could do such a thing. She would have called the gardaí if she had made the connection.

In any event, John Mulhall Snr appeared to Marie to know nothing about it, and they moved on to talking about more mundane matters. Marie would later make a statement which read:

'I discussed the news story with my father, John. We just had a short conversation about it. He did not seem to know anything about the body at that stage.'

CHAPTER THREE

'Every murder turns on a bright hot light, and a lot of people have to walk out of the shadows.'

- *Albert Maltz, writer,* The Naked City

THE TASK OF removing the body parts began at 8.30am the following morning. However, this was complicated by the fact that divers from the Garda Sub-Aqua Unit had to map out the exact locations of the body parts in the canal and retrieve any forensic evidence present.

The canal was 1.8 metres deep under the bridge, which made the job even more difficult. It should also be noted that Noor's torso had already been taken from the water by this stage by two officers, Brian Breathnach and Eoin Ferriter. They began removing the smaller body parts that were visible from the bank around 9.55am after they had surveyed the scene.

It was clear from the start that those tasked with investigating the killing understood the importance of gathering as much vital evidence as possible. To ensure this goal was achieved, an underwater video camera was erected to document the search for forensic evidence.

The process was slow, and in many ways revolting. The body parts were in an advanced state of decomposition; the flesh was brittle to the touch and came off the bone easily when disturbed. The garda divers had to be careful when handling the remains for this reason.

In total, the divers found seven body parts in the water directly under Clarke's Bridge. Each one of these was placed in a special plastic bag while still underwater, to preserve it, and then brought to the surface; a process which took hours.

Even though no post-mortem examination had taken place to show how the victim had died, the brutality of the act was obvious to all. There was no doubt that this had been a savage killing— perhaps the most savage the detectives had ever investigated.

The torso, they could easily see, was peppered with stab wounds, dozens of them, from which little water creatures emerged.

When the bags containing the body parts had been removed from the canal, they were collected by the Dublin firm of undertakers, Staffords, and taken to Beaumont Hospital in north Dublin, where they were x-rayed, before being transported to the city's morgue for a post-mortem examination.

It should be noted that the body parts were contained in two separate bags. Few of the pathology staff and the gardaí who received them had ever experienced anything like it. There were seven body parts in total but the absence of the head was very much to the front of the detectives' minds.

This caused many of those present to ponder as to what exactly had happened. All felt there was something deeply saddening about the murder, which was lost on many of the journalists who reported on the death. The victim had not just been murdered; his remains had been denigrated in a most brutal fashion. This feeling hung like an ominous shadow over the body parts.

Behind the bloodshed and the grisly way the victim's body had been disposed of, there was a person, and possibly a family. This fact was not lost on those on the investigation team, who ordered the body parts to be treated with a great degree of respect, similar to that shown to a body.

The post-mortem examination began in the evening when Dr Michael Curtis, the deputy state pathologist, arrived at the Dublin City Morgue. The purpose of the post-mortem itself was to establish whether the victim had been murdered, or had, for some reason, been dismembered after dying of natural causes. None of the detectives assembled thought about discounting the latter scenario; it was unlikely, but it was something they could not rule out.

Among those assembled to witness the first examination of the body were the team whose job it would be to first identify the victim, and then track down the killers. Overall responsibility for investigating the crime rested with the District Detective Unit attached to Fitzgibbon Street Station. However, they were joined by detectives from nearby Store Street and Mountjoy Garda Stations, and also the National Bureau of Criminal Investigation, who had been seconded to assist.

The actual responsibility for the inquiry rested with the local detective team led by Christy Mangan, a detective inspector. He was a police officer who took a direct approach to his job; he didn't suffer fools gladly and tended to deal with people in a straight, no nonsense way. He knew the streets, the shady characters that inhabited

Dublin's underworld, and how the wheels of justice turned.

However, Mangan had never overseen a murder inquiry where a body had been dismembered, but few in the Garda had. The one personality trait he possessed that would stand to him was his fervent belief in maintaining an open mind at all times on everything.

While every member of the team had of course investigated countless murders, it was obvious that the torso in the canal was no ordinary killing. It was evident to all that whoever the victim was, he had suffered an unimaginable death. Among the crimes and atrocities that had convulsed Ireland, this—the dismemberment of a body—stood out as horrific, virulent and cruel. Though they all knew they were dealing with a violent death, and possibly something far more sinister, the dismemberment presented so many questions that the post-mortem took on a special urgency.

*****

The procedure itself began at 7.40pm that evening and consisted of a thorough examination of what remained of the corpse in the beleaguered hope that it could determine the cause and manner of death.

Working methodically, Dr Curtis removed the various body parts from the two bags. Those present in the room were all struck by the smell of decomposition, which was at times overpowering.

It should be noted that no one knew whether the victim was black or white at this stage; there had been a degree of epidermal separation, which had turned the victim's flesh white, disguising his race, and his likely country of origin.

In accordance with procedure, each of the body parts was first measured and photographed. When this task was complete, the pathologist began an external examination of the remains. This was carried out in a forensic fashion; he noted the various segments and the kind of clothes found with the dismembered remains.

Of course, the most obvious missing parts of the body were the head and the victim's penis. The pathologist also noted there were a number of items of clothing found. There was the white-coloured Ireland jersey, but there was also a vest, a white checked towel and a pair of socks. These were looked at closely.

In many ways it was a difficult post-mortem. For a start, the body was contaminated with silt and fresh water prawns, which fed on the flesh, particularly around the wounds. These hampered the speed of the examination.

The pathologist next took a description of the body as best he could. He noted the sex and other distinguishing features, which could help identify the victim, but these proved elusive given the dismemberment. The dissection of the body, brutal and hurried as it was, had had the desired effect, insofar that it made parts of the post-mortem difficult. Dr Curtis, though, persevered.

He then examined each body part. One of the first examined in detail was the upper torso. The pathologist noticed it still contained most of the soft tissue that surrounds the abdomen. The examination of this body part revealed in excess of 22 stab wounds to the upper torso in the front and rear. There were also three cuts to the back. Whoever had stabbed the victim had done so with enormous ferocity.

Judging the shape of the wounds, the pathologist guessed the weapon was some type of sharp knife, possibly a kitchen knife.

Once the torso was examined, he moved on to the right and left upper limbs. These, he proclaimed to the detectives, had been divided at the level of the upper humerus on each side. He had never seen anything like it in his career.

Another body part that yielded some more clues was the lower torso, which still contained the hip joints. The pathologist recorded that a pair of white underpants were present on these.

Below the pants, he found the penis of the victim had been cut off, along with an anterior part of the scrotum. This was a barbaric act by any standard.

He also noted the upper femora had been divided. In fact, the detached thighs had been divided just above the knee. Both lower limbs were there as well, with the feet intact. He noted the presence of grey-charcoal socks on each foot.

The body was next cleaned, weighed and measured in preparation for an internal examination. This was to be unique insofar as the chest was easier to cut open, showing maximum exposure of the trunk. This part of the post-mortem consisted of inspecting the internal organs of the body parts for evidence of trauma, or other indications of the cause of death.

Dr Curtis began this by making a large and deep Y-shaped incision from shoulder to shoulder, meeting at the breastbone and extending all the way down to the abdomen. The chest plate was opened, so that the heart and lungs could be seen.

At this stage of the medical process, the organs were left exposed. From close inspection of the wounds, he confirmed a sharp knife had been used to stab the victim. While the soft tissue around the bones had been severed clumsily by repeated blows or chopping from an axe or cleaver, the incisions into the flesh were smooth.

He found that virtually all of the internal organs—the heart, lungs, kidneys and bladder—had been injured in the assault that had taken the victim's life. When he examined all of the sections together, he noted that the head, penis and cervical spine were absent.

Mangan did not discount the importance of this particular information, which suggested that a personal grudge, possibly of a sexual nature, may have been the motive for the killing.

When Dr Curtis had finished his examination, he concluded the victim had died from numerous stab wounds; he was then dismembered. Part of his job was to give the team an idea of what type of man they were looking for.

He was able to make some calculations on the victim's height, race and age with some simple calculations. He assembled all the body parts on the post-mortem table; they measured 5 feet 4 inches. He concluded that the victim would have been about six feet tall in life.

The post-mortem was unique insofar as Dr Curtis could not perform a reconstitution of the body, such that it could be viewed, if desired, by relatives of the deceased, if they were ever found.

This was exactly the type of information that Mangan required although, in truth, the post-mortem didn't reveal many clues about the victim's identity. However it did provide the detectives with an idea about how he died. The most noticeable aspect was that there were no defensive injuries on the hands. Whoever the victim was, he had probably been taken by surprise, and most likely knew his killers.

*****

It was not the first time a corpse had been found in the Royal Canal in the north inner city. Cold blooded killers had used the waterway to dump the bodies of their victims in the past. Four years earlier, in July 2001, youths had found a suitcase in the exact same stretch of canal, which contained the bruised and bloodied body of a Romanian national named Adrian Bestia. He had been just 23 years old when he was murdered.

The discovery of Noor's remains, though, was starkly different from an investigators point of view, for the simple fact that whoever had killed him had gone to great lengths to disguise his identity. It wasn't, however, the first time that gardaí dealt with a headless corpse. In July 2004, less than a year prior to Noor's remains being discovered, a headless body was found beside a stream near Piltown, a village in Co. Kilkenny. The victim was a 25-year-old Malawi woman named Paiche Onyemaechi. She was a mother of two and daughter of the Chief Justice of Malawi, Leonard Unyolo. Her head was never found.

She was identified by cross-checking her fingerprints against the asylum-seeker database, which contains prints taken from all asylum seekers who have entered Ireland since November 2001. As Noor had arrived in Ireland in 1996, checking his fingerprints against this database yielded no information, although gardaí were hopeful his fingerprints could be matched with a set on the Garda database.

The only other case of dismemberment encountered by the Garda was over 40 years ago. In 1963 a medical student, Shan Mohangi, had murdered and dismembered his 16-year-old girlfriend Hazel Mullen, before boiling her remains in the basement of a restaurant on Harcourt Street in Dublin city.

The prosecution of Mohangi was a relatively straightforward affair though, as he was caught at the scene with the dissected body. In this case, the detective team didn't even know whose murder they were investigating.

Through the post-mortem examination, it had been established that the body was that of a black male, so gardaí began canvassing members of the ethnic community in Dublin.

This became the focus of the immediate inquiry. The problem that Mangan faced was where to find a missing man, possibly an immigrant, in a city where immigrants used various names and changed identities regularly.

If this crime were to be solved, it would be through old fashioned investigation techniques, and not luck.

In the hours that followed the extraction of the body parts from the water, Mangan had set up an incident room in the station. He wanted this to act as a nerve centre for the inquiry, but also as an interface, where the public could pass on relevant information.

Among the assembled team were Detective Sergeant Gerry McDonnell, Detective Garda Dave O'Brien, Detective Garda Adrian Murray and Detective Garda Dan Kenna, who began to compile statements that would be used in the book of evidence.

From the beginning, the team made a conscious decision to use the press to encourage those with any information to come forward. This was relatively easy because the discovery of the body parts had continued to dominate the news headlines. When the follow-up searches of the canal failed to locate the victim's head; interest in the inquiry soared. The question remained: where was the victim's head?

Behind the fanfare of media speculation, the investigation team got to work. The inquiry initially took various forms, but the prime focus was to identify the victim.

Hence, the problem the team faced was not how to find evidence that could secure a conviction, but how to find evidence to identify him. The damage to the body parts was such that it yielded no forensic evidence that could be used in a future trial.

Left with no other option, Mangan circulated a description of the victim, as far as it was possible, to security agencies across Europe. The details were checked against the Garda missing persons register, and the details of the find and likely height of the victim were circulated to Interpol. DNA samples had been taken from the body parts and these were checked against existing databases.

Mangan and others on the team also gave interviews to *The Metro* and *The Street* newspapers, hoping it might prompt someone with information to come forward. They also spoke to religious figures in the African community living in the greater Dublin area. To complement this effort, the team produced posters in a number of different languages, appealing for anyone with information to come forward.

These posters, which displayed the white soccer jersey found with the torso, and the underwear, were circulated. The Crimestoppers organisation also offered a reward of €10,000.

This move generated a significant response insofar as names of various people and missing persons were nominated in secret calls to the incident room, but these were quickly ruled out. In spite of everything, the identity of the victim proved itself to be an elusive and evasive quarry.

*****

Not far away—in the same city—Linda Mulhall had begun to panic. She had suffered from panic attacks ever since she was a child. Now when she closed her eyes, she was haunted by Noor's face. She couldn't stop thinking about what she'd done; how she'd covered his head before cutting it from his body.

The utter violence of the death that she and Charlotte had visited upon the victim did not fade from her memory; it grew until she could think of nothing else. It was this feeling—one of being haunted by the memory of Noor—which drove her to return, under the cover of darkness, to where they had buried his head in the Sean Walsh Memorial Park.

Though it may have been because she didn't trust Charlotte, and didn't want her to know what she was about to do, she decided to move it to another location.

In a statement she later made to gardaí, she recalled sitting on the bench close to where the head was buried. Here, she prayed and prayed, hoping that somehow the nightmare would end. More than anything, she was terrified that someone would notice the head buried in the ground. The truth was that someone already had.

A member of the public had seen the head when he sat on the bench in the park some days after the discovery of the headless, dismembered body. Laurence Keegan, a retired army private, went to the park alone every day to drink and smoke. He sat on the same bench in the same location. A few days after the discovery in the Royal Canal, he was sitting on his usual bench in the park when he noticed what he thought was the top of a head with short dark hair protruding from the ground. He tried to dig it out of the ground with the toe of his boots, but failed. It occurred to him that what he was looking at may have been the head of the body from the canal.

He told his daughter what he had seen and asked her to return to the park to help him dig it up, but she didn't believe him and refused. He saw the head there for a few more days and then it disappeared.

At the time, this was unknown to Linda. She put her hands on what appeared to be a rock but was in fact Noor's head. It was now smooth and hairless. As she lifted the body part from its resting place, she tried not to look at it; she simply couldn't. What went through her mind can only be surmised.

According to her own statement, she placed the head into a black plastic bag and concealed it in bushes in Killinarden Park until the next day. When she returned, she brought her son's empty school bag on her back.

Carefully, she put the head into the school bag and walked as far as Brittas. She had lived in Brittas for a while, so she was familiar with the area. She trembled as she walked and tried to remain in control, though it was clear that she was in fact beginning to lose her senses.

Once she took possession of Noor's head, she found that she couldn't function without alcohol. So on that morning, she brought a litre of vodka with her, which she hoped would give her the strength to do what she needed to do.

Once she had walked through Brittas, she made her way out into the countryside and away from the sprawl of the housing estates. She then walked deep into a field until she was out of sight.

Here, she fell to her knees, kissed the bag and told Noor that she was sorry. In many ways she was. At that moment, she wanted all the pain that she was experiencing to go away.

She was now beyond grief and despair. She drank the bottle of vodka and spent a few hours sitting with the head. She spoke to the victim, pleaded with him to forgive her, and said she wished she could go back in time. Her mind was full of suicidal thoughts which she dared not admit. She then took the hammer out of the bag and began to smash what remained of the head, trying to break it up into smaller pieces.

In her drunken state, she fell asleep with the smashed head lying beside her. When she woke up, she was cold, and it was getting dark. She saw a mucky patch on the ground beside her and once again attempted to hide the head. She covered the evidence with soil, and said a prayer over it.

Linda was filled with remorse as she whispered to what remained of Noor: 'I'm sorry. It should not be you.'

When she had covered the head as best she could, she lit a small fire and burned the black plastic bag and the schoolbag there in the field. She ran all the way home, where she fell into bed, exhausted and emotionally wasted.

*****

In the days following the brutal death of Noor, according to statements made to gardaí, Kathleen reported that he was still alive but had left her.

By a stroke of good fortune, Noor had been absent from his place of work at Schmitt ECS on the Friday prior to his death, causing an official at the Adecco Recruitment Agency, which had secured him the job, to try track him down. The company had failed to locate him but one of the staff had managed to contact Kathleen, who allegedly gave the excuse that Noor was away minding a sick baby, and she did not know where he was, nor when he would be back.

The day after the killing, a recruitment consultant with Adecco Recruitment Agency once again attempted to contact Noor but failed. She too called Kathleen, who Noor often referred to as 'the boss', on her mobile phone.

The agency did not have any reason to question Kathleen's response to the query. She didn't sound nervous and she told the company that she was no longer involved with Noor. Speaking without fear of contradiction, she said he 'had moved to Kilkenny with a young one.'

No one noticed anything unusual about Kathleen's behaviour in the days after the killing. Instead she allegedly told anyone who would listen that Noor had left her for another woman.

John Tobin, one witness later interviewed by the investigation team, recalled collecting rent on 25 March. He recalled that she had casually remarked that Noor had left her and had gone back to live with a girl who had a baby with him. He referred to Kathleen as Katherine.

'Katherine said to me that Farah had left her. He had gone back to a girl that had a baby for him. Katherine had said that she only lived around the corner. She never mentioned the girl's name. Katherine had said that Farah had a few children in Cork. Katherine told me that Farah was working, I think it was security on nights, maybe a clothes shop, I'm not sure. She found out that he wasn't working there half the time and that he was seeing this other girl. She told me that some of Farah's stuff was in black bags downstairs, I think I noticed two or three bags.'

A number of witnesses reported hearing similar stories from Kathleen. Sometime after the killing, a friend of Noor's called Ibrahim Mohamed met her at 77 Upper Gardiner Street. She also asked him had he seen Noor because she was looking for him.

It looks like she was trying to ensure that anyone who came looking for Noor would think they had separated. It is likely that she was trying to put distance between herself and the killing.

By this stage she had moved to erase all evidence of what had taken place in the flat at Richmond Cottages. This included disposing of the blood stained carpet and replacing it with a new one.

On 26 March, she purchased a piece of carpet for €50 at the Carpet Mills on Thomas Street. The sale was made by Joseph Eustace and delivery was made to 17 Richmond Cottages days later. The old carpet was discarded until she could find a way to dispose of it.

It is probable that Kathleen knew that although the body parts had been found, the team had still not managed to identify the victim. And no one suspected a thing.

She may have thought that she could, by then, relax. However, witnesses reported that she continued to say that Noor had left her. Around this time, she rang Ali Suleiman Abdulaziz, another friend of Noor's, enquiring about him. When Abdulaziz asked her if Noor was still living with her, she refused to say anything, and hung up.

No one thought for a moment that Noor had been killed, but Abdulaziz began to think he may be in trouble. Out of concern, he rang Kathleen three or four days later. Abdulaziz told gardaí that when he asked if Noor had returned, she said, 'Ali, I'm finished with Farah.'

CHAPTER FOUR

'Everything that deceives may be said to enchant.'

- Plato

PERHAPS THE GREATEST, yet an unforeseen problem, encountered by Mangan and the detective team was the general assumption that Noor had been murdered as part of a ritual sacrifice.

Noor's death had had a powerful impact on the citizens of Dublin, if not the entire country. The details of how the body had been dismembered—that the head could not be found—created a moral dilemma for the investigators. The last thing they wanted the public to believe was that this was an unsolvable crime, or a killing that didn't concern them. In this regard, the team could not reveal any clues that might insinuate this was a ritual killing. In truth, they had no idea what had happened. And the inquiries were further complicated by the fact that witnesses started to present themselves to the team, stating categorically, that the killing *was* ritual. At one stage, the team were told by one witness that a killer had come to Ireland, performed the ritual, then returned to Africa. The fact that the head had still not been located appeared to support this theory, although the team figured it was just as likely that whoever was responsible wanted them to think it was a ritual killing.

Mangan, though, decided that no one would be drawn into any line of specific inquiry, although the team knew they could not discount the ritual sacrifice theory. He was of the opinion that the public would ignore their pleas for help if they thought this was a matter involving immigrants. The truth was that no one, certainly in Ireland, knew anything about ritual killing, black magic or the occult for that matter.

They were also aware of the possible backlash if they attempted to explore this line of inquiry without proper advice; it would open a Pandora's Box of justified criticism. This is why they chose to approach experts in the field.

Through the offices of the international liaison department in Garda Headquarters, Mangan approached Superintendent Gerard Labuschagne of the Ritual Killing Unit of the South African Police Force in Pretoria. Through official channels, the team passed the specific details on the killing to the South African Police, who examined the paperwork with a keen interest.

In sanctioned correspondence, Labuschagne's officials began to dictate what their Irish counterparts needed to bear in mind, if they were indeed investigating a *muti* killing. In many ways, this was a turning point in the investigation: their advice was not to accept anything at face value.

To the detectives on the torso in the canal team; it was hard to imagine killings that involved the abduction, murder and dismemberment of a victim with the aim of obtaining body parts for use in traditional medicine. In contrast to their own expectations, they were told that such killings took place in the darkest of subterfuge. *Muti* murders were not hastily arranged, but carefully planned; they had to be.

The consensus reached by the South African Police was that the gardaí were probably not dealing with *muti*, or certainly not a true ritual killing carried out by someone with knowledge of *muti*. If it had been, other parts of the body, not just the head and penis, would have been harvested. In *muti*, body parts of victims were sometimes eaten, drunk or smeared on the person wishing to avail of the victim's powers. Therefore, if the killers were *muti* killers, it was logical to assume they either wanted to become more intelligent or increase their sexual prowess.

The advice received from South Africa, however, showed that *muti* killings, almost always, involved the harvesting of organs while the victim was alive. The reason for this was simple: practitioners of human sacrifice believe the screams of their victims make the *muti* more powerful.

The experts did concede that some elements of the canal case seemed to point to *muti*. Typically the victim's of *muti* were disembowelled, and body parts were removed from the inside of the body as well as, in most cases, the genitalia.

The three cuts in the torso's back were also similar to those found on *muti* victims.

There was yet another factor that had to be considered. Britain had experienced *muti* killings. In 2001, the Metropolitan Police in London found a torso in the Thames River. The subsequent inquiry revealed the torso to be that of a young, African boy who had been murdered. The investigation never discovered the true identity of the boy but named the child 'Adam'. That particular inquiry led to West Africa and the arrests of scores of people across Europe, including Ireland, but the killer was never located.

However, some of the techniques used in the 'Adam' investigation were adopted by the Dublin team.

In London, a technique called Isotope Analysis was used to establish the nationality of the dead boy. This involved testing samples from his intestines to reconstruct diet, and oxygen isotopes to determine geographic origin. The Garda were keen to do the same as, although they now knew the victim was black, they still had no idea where he came from or who the victim was. For this task, they hired the services of a forensic geologist in Belfast called Dr Auguestin. His techniques were similar to those used to test bone recovered from archaeological sites. These could be analysed isotopically for information regarding diet and migration while sometimes tooth enamel and soil clinging to remains could also be used in isotope analysis.

In theory, it was possible to at least identify the victim's country of origin, but in practice it was a less than exact science.

Mangan had hoped he might get a breakthrough using this technique; though he was soon to learn that fortune was to pay him a favour. Two witnesses had come forward.

*****

On Monday, 9 May, some six weeks after the body parts had first been discovered in the canal, Noor's friend from Kismayu, Mohammed Ali Abu Bakaar read an article a newspaper called *The Street Journal.* That he was reading the article was a chance occurrence. The story in question told of how the dismembered remains of a black male had been found in the Royal Canal.

The article quoted Mangan talking about the investigation, how the body had been found, and the urgent need for help.

The article in itself didn't attract Bakaar's interest; he merely glanced at the contents. What did was the photograph that accompanied it. It showed a white Ireland football jersey, the same type of jersey he had seen his friend Farah Noor wearing during the St Patrick's weekend celebrations. The more Bakaar read, the more he became concerned, though initially he didn't panic. Noor had been in the company of his girlfriend, Kathleen. If anything had happened; surely she would have reported him missing.

As a precaution more than anything else, he tried to call Noor on his mobile phone, but the line was disconnected. He thought this was strange. He then inquired among members of the Somali community living in Dublin. No one had heard from Noor for some time.

When he spoke to Deirdre Hyland, the woman who had also met Noor on O'Connell Street in March, she too became anxious.

Like everyone else, the two had heard about the grotesque killing but they did not wish to waste police time. The two were calm and lucid, and thought about what best to do.

Rather than call the incident room directly, Hyland called a cousin in the Garda who passed on their concerns to Fitzgibbon Street. This was the first breakthrough in the torso in the canal case.

When the team heard that two witnesses had come forward, they became excited. The information, though, took on a fresh urgency once Mangan was discreetly informed the potential victim had been seen wearing an Irish soccer jersey. Two detectives—Malachy Dunne and Patrick Flood—were immediately sent to interview the witnesses about what they had seen.

By this stage, other people from the immigrant community had also become concerned for Noor.

Another friend of his, Mohammed Ali Noor, had come forward to say he had also met him around St Patrick's Day and he read the newspaper articles. He too had expressed his concerns to a mutual friend, Rashid Omar Ahmed, and asked him to inquire around Dublin and Cork to see if anyone had seen Noor. None had.

But it was Bakaar's information that proved to be of particular value. He recalled meeting his old fishing friend with a woman he named as Katherine, who was his long term girlfriend.

His recollection of the day he met Noor, the conversation they shared, and specifically the clothes he had been wearing, were clearly accurate. The more the detectives heard, the more convinced they were that they had the right man.

Mangan was inclined to agree.

Hours after the initial contact with Bakaar was made, a member of the team conducted a cursory check on the Garda intelligence system: PULSE. This yielded more information; Noor was already known to them. Although he had been convicted for some public order offences, this didn't interest them.

It was information pertaining to the murder of Raonaid Murray, a 16-year-old girl found stabbed to death near her home in Dun Laoghaire, which caused them to wonder; not alone had Noor been nominated as a possible killer; he had been formally interviewed.

The catalogue of intelligence on the missing man made interesting reading. It gave specific information on Noor, detailing his past acquaintances, arrival in Ireland, personal history and habits.

Noor had first arrived in Ireland on 30 December 1996. In early January 1997, he lodged an application for refugee status with the Department of Justice in the name of Farah Swaleh Noor.

In his dealings with officials, he claimed to have been born in the Somali capital of Mogadishu on 2 July 1967, where he worked as a fisherman with the Department of Fisheries in Kismayu. This particular piece of information corroborated Bakaar's story, further strengthening his information.

The reason for his flight to Ireland had been apparently straightforward. He said he had a wife and three children who had been murdered during the civil war that had engulfed Somalia.

In his dealings with the Department of Justice, he specifically mentioned that he'd found his wife shot dead, causing him to flee to Kenya.

The story continued. His file stated that he had lived in Kenya for five years before he agreed to pay an agent $1,600 to get him on board a flight to Europe.

Officials from the Department of Justice had called him for interview on 2 June 1998. On that occasion, he spoke through an interpreter, though it was clear he could speak English when he wanted to. In that interview, he said he had no idea where his family were, and no idea how to find his parents. The drama of the story didn't end there. He next answered a series of questions on the political situation in Somalia and stated that he was terrified of returning home, saying he would be killed by guerrillas if forced to leave Ireland. It was noted that he spoke convincingly about life in a refugee camp, the political situation that consumed Somalia, and the effects this had on his family.

The intelligence information intrigued the team. The story was one of heroic bravery in the face of adversity. He had also claimed he was forced to flee from Kenya because he was a member of an ethnic minority, the Bajun. When the opportunity to flee came, he took it, because he had no other choice.

The file noted that Noor was further interviewed on 17 September that same year, again through an interpreter. On this occasion, he showed his interviewers faded scars that appeared on his wrist,

Right: Linda Mulhall, a mother of four, who always considered herself to be in the wrong place at the wrong time. She broke down several times when making statements to detectives about the killing of Farah Swaleh Noor, but pleaded not guilty when the case went to court.

© Collins Agency / Chris Maddaloni

© Collins Agency / Chris Maddaloni

Left: Charlotte Mulhall, nicknamed 'Charlie' by her sister, was the younger of the two dubbed the 'Scissor Sisters', after details of their horrific crime came to light.

The brutal killing of the victim shocked the media and public alike, and was considered one of the most violent cases in the history of the state.

Above: Farah Swaleh Noor, also known as Sheilila Salim, with an ex-girlfriend, with whom he had a son (**right**).

With this woman's co-operation, the Garda were able to match the child's DNA with that found on the torso in the canal, formally identifying the victim. They later matched this DNA with that found at the scene of the killing.

Above: The section of the Royal Canal at Ballybough Bridge where the dismembered torso was discovered, is in the shadow of Croke Park.

Above and below: Forensic gardaí and the Garda Sub Aqua Unit removed seven body parts from the canal. The dismembered body was so badly decomposed that the flesh fell from the bone at the slightest touch, and evidence had to be placed in bags underwater to preserve them as much as possible.

© Photocall Ireland / Leon Farrell

Above: Some of the items found with the body parts included a pair of socks and Y-fronts, but it was hoped that the distinctive Ireland 'away' jersey would be key in identifying the victim. This proved to be the case.

Right: From left to right, Superintendent John Leahy and Detective Inspector Christy Mangan talk to the media about the discovery of the remains in the Royal Canal. At first it was thought that this could have been a ritual killing, as the head had not been found.

© Photocall Ireland / Leon Farrell

Murder of a black male, information required.

CRIMESTOPPERS

Reward Offered

Gardai at Fitzgibbon Street are investigating the murder of a black male whose decapitated and dismembered body was found in the Royal Canal at Ballybough Bridge, Dublin 3, on Wednesday the 30th of March 2005. The victim may have been in the water for one to two weeks. He may have been missing since before St. Patricks Day, 17th of March 2005. To date the head of the victim has not been located and his identity is unknown.

The victim is described as:

* A black male possibly African
* Aged 20s – 40 years
* Strong Build
* Possibly 6ft plus in height
* A distinctive long sleeved Ireland (away) jersey was found with the torso

Crimestoppers are making available a substantial cash reward for specific imformation leading to the identity of the victim and the person or persons responsible for his murder.

Any information to:

CRIMESTOPPERS

Freephone **1800-25 00 25**

or

 Incident room at Fitzgibbon Street

Freephone **1800-218 219**

Above: The Crimestoppers appeal for information to help identify the victim found dismembered in the canal included the distinctive clothes found with the body in the hope that they might jog a witness's memory.

ight: 17 Richmond ottages, Ballybough, here the gruesome lling and dismem- erment of Farah waleh Noor took ace.

Gardaí discovered aces of blood there, en after Kathleen ulhall, Linda and harlotte's mother, d moved out. It took tween six and eight ours for the body to chopped up in the hall bathroom of this nner city flat.

© Collins Agency / Arthur Carron

© Collins Agency / Chris Maddaloni

© Collins Agency / Garrett White

Charlotte and Linda made conflicting statements to detectives when questioned about what had happened on the night Noor was killed. Weeks after denying any knowledge of Noor's death, a distraught Linda contacted detectives to confess to the killing.

Above: Marie Mulhall, who offered to make a statement to detectives detailing her sister Charlotte's confession to the killing. She would later give evidence at the trial.

Above: John Mulhall Snr, who encouraged his daughters to confes to the killing. He tragically committed suicide in December 2005, shortly after Linda and Charlotte were arrested and charged.

which he said were caused after he was assaulted by a group of bandits or soldiers.

This time, none of the officials believed his story. On 15 December his application for refugee status was rejected on the grounds that he was lying. He was informed of this decision on 2 February 1999, but he didn't accept the decision.

Nine days later, he lodged an appeal and was re-interviewed on 3 June 1999. Some three weeks later, the Appeals Authority recommended that he be allowed to stay. It was a good result for Noor, considering the fact that he wasn't even a Somali.

The story had been a tissue of lies; Noor was in fact a Kenyan. He had lied about his nationality, and even the death of his wife and children, to gain political asylum.

*****

While the details of his asylum process gave the investigation an insight into the potential victim, it was the contact name of a past girlfriend that held the key to solving the crime. This woman had been forced to contact the Garda in fear of her life. This fact was in itself not important; it was her son, or more specifically, his DNA.

The woman in question had previously been in a relationship with Noor. According to the realms of intelligence on PULSE, Noor had threatened her, forcing her to seek protection.

The inquiry team wasted no time in trying to locate this potential witness.

On 20 May, two officers called out to the woman's home in south Dublin having spent hours trying to track her down. Like everyone else, she had watched the news bulletins on the grim discovery of the body parts, but thought nothing more of it. The visit of two detectives caught her by surprise, as she would later recall:

'I was at home one day and two gardaí came to the door. They had a picture of an Ireland jersey and asked if Farah ever wore clothes like it. I said he did.

'At that point, and I still remember it to this day, one of them said, "We think it may be him." I froze because I just knew it was him. I just knew. I was shocked. I suppose it was the manner in which he was killed.'

The purpose of the visit was to take some DNA samples from her son, to confirm the identification of Noor. This was the only accurate way of determining for sure whether Noor had been killed. She consented immediately but her heart told her that Noor was already dead. 'I had a gut feeling,' she said.

When she recovered from the initial shock, she spoke freely about her relationship with Noor. She had perhaps known him more intimately than anyone else.

They had spent three years together, and had had a baby boy. For that reason alone, she was invaluable, but she knew more, as she would later recall in an interview:

'I first met Farah when I was 16 years old. I was in third year in school. I was only a school girl. I actually met him when I was walking through town with my friends one day. He came over and started talking to me.

'He told me he was 20. He was very charming at first. We started going out and it became very serious fast. I suppose now I realise it was puppy love but at the time it was very real.'

The relationship blossomed. The two became an item. Three months later, she got pregnant.

'He didn't get me pregnant just to claim asylum. He was very careful not to be seen to have a relationship with me just for that. Instead he became part of my family. He would spend a lot of time in my parents' home and he became part of our family. You could say he was a full member of my family.'

Noor loved and cherished their child. While he was a Muslim, he allowed his partner to have her son baptised a Catholic; his religious beliefs were never an issue. After two years they decided to move in together.

'We got a flat in Dublin and everything was great. I suppose you could say it was good for a period of time. Then he began to change.'

Much of what Noor told the mother of his son were lies. For a start, he was a chronic alcoholic, who had already been married in Kenya. He was also a father of three children, whom he had abandoned. He kept the existence of this relationship, in fact all matters pertaining to his previous life, a secret.

Perhaps the true measure of his duplicity could be gauged from the absolute conviction he showed every time he said his wife had died. Most of what he said was untrue; Farah Swaleh Noor was not even his name; he was born Sheilila Salim.

This was irrelevant to his young lover who didn't care; she knew him and loved him for being Farah. The relationship was mostly normal until they moved in together, as she would tell:

'I remember what happened the first time that things started to go seriously wrong. I was out with my friend and he started saying that one of my friends was a lesbian, who wanted to sleep with me. I just stood there, thinking that I was hearing things. He kept shouting abuse at my friend saying that she wanted me. It was stupid. That night I was too afraid to go home so I stayed with a friend.

'The next day I went back home and he beat me. This happened every few days from that day onwards. Then the sexual violence started.'

Noor raped the mother of his child on a frequent basis, every few days. He disregarded her objections to sex out of hand.

'He would just force himself on me—no matter how much I'd resist. He would force me to be with him and would never take no for an answer. This happened every day. It was a nightmare. I thought this was normal because I was very young. I also had a baby to care for and I just was too young to handle the situation. I also didn't want to admit that I'd made a mistake.'

The relationship that started out as a loving and caring one now turned into a living hell; Noor beat her on a daily basis.

'I left him twice but when I came back he'd beat me up. He'd then say he was sorry. When he'd hit me, I would fight back. It got so bad that I began to tell my friends and they demanded that I do something. One of them said she'd call my parents if I didn't leave him and in the end, that's what happened. She did.'

Her parents were shocked and horrified to hear the truth. No one had suspected a thing. Alcoholism now consumed Noor. It was not unusual for him to drink 3 litres of vodka a week. This inevitably forced him to lead a dysfunctional life.

'When my parents found out, my Dad came down and collected me. I had been with him from 1998 to 2001. My father and mother could not believe what had been happening because they had treated Farah like one of their own. They were upset. They had no idea of the way he was treating me.'

Despite his own behaviour and violence, Noor refused to accept the relationship was over. He continued to visit his son every week in the hope of rebuilding the relationship.

'Farah, he was a good father. He was a very loving father to his son and doted on him. He had his own problems with alcohol but I don't think he was evil or anything like that. He just changed when he drank alcohol. It made him into a different man. There was a time when he was the nicest bloke in the world, but he turned into something else when he drank.'

His attitude to women continued to deteriorate, however. Alcohol only accelerated this. When the relationship ended, he refused to take no for an answer. It was at this point that he began threatening her.

'He started to follow me around. Everywhere I went he would just turn up. He'd come to the house but then he'd hang around the area. If I went to the shops, he'd be there. If I went out for a drink, he'd turn up at the bar. I was afraid of him. I knew what he was capable of,' she said referring to the rapes.

It was during the bitter break-up that Noor made references to the stabbing of Raonaid Murray, the young teenager whose death had convulsed Ireland. One night, while in a drunken rage, he implied that he was her killer. She later recalled the scene:

'There were three of us outside a pub. He knew one of my friends had known Raonaid Murray and he started shouting: "You're the reason why she's dead." My friend went straight to the gardaí because he was trying to suggest he was the killer.'

She eventually sought and secured a protection order keeping him away from her home, but this didn't work. Instead it was a new relationship she entered into that drove Noor away.

'When I met my husband, he virtually vanished. He knew there was no point, that I had met someone else. He didn't even come to see our son. It was over.'

The conversation she shared with the detectives revealed more clues. She too mentioned Kathleen Mulhall, specifically that she had called her saying Noor was beating her.

'She had started to call me asking for help. She said that Farah was beating her. She was very upset and was looking for help. I didn't really know what to say because I had moved on, but she seemed desperate.

'She asked me for advice. I remember one time, when she called late at night; she said she had got my telephone number from his phone. She was looking for advice. I advised her to leave him. I said he would never change. She wanted to know had he ever beaten me or attacked me. I told her the full story, and urged her to leave. I told her about the abuse.'

Kathleen, she said, always called late at night and was polite.

'On one occasion, she told me she was pregnant and that she was calling because she knew I was also pregnant.

'But I later found out that she never was. She knew I was in a new relationship but I told her to leave him. I remember telling her that he would never change and that something awful would happen if she didn't.'

That was the last call. She never heard from Kathleen after that. This didn't perturb her too much, for obvious reasons.

As the gardaí chatted to her in the living room of her council home, they next found out that Noor and his girlfriend had moved to Cork for a time. The woman said she had last seen him in September 2002, almost a year after the relationship ended.

This evidence was crucial, but her son was vital. If the torso and body parts found in the canal were indeed those of Noor, it would be his son's DNA that could confirm it. The detectives thanked her for her time and then took a DNA swab from her son's mouth. It was a simple process that could solve a complex case. As they left, they said they'd be in touch.

*****

Once Bakaar and Hyland made their statements, Linda and Charlotte Mulhall, and their mother, Kathleen, became suspects. This led detectives to the flat at Richmond Cottages on 21 May. When members of the team knocked at the door, they were told Kathleen had moved out. While this was not proof of any crime, it suggested that something had happened, at least—that she and Noor were no longer together.

In a strange twist of fortune, the fact that Kathleen had vacated the premises assisted the investigation team, as they were permitted entry to the flat by the new tenant Caitriona Burke, who lived there with her three-year-old son. She had thought nothing of moving into the flat and agreed to help the Garda in any way she could. The detectives asked if she had noticed anything unusual. Her answer was honest: she hadn't. Though, when she thought back, she did recall a big blue ring on the floor at the bedroom door, and some missing carpet.

The missing carpet had been discovered by chance. When she had moved a double bed, she saw there was no carpet but just a concrete floor.

'It was like it was just patched up to give the impression that there was carpet on the floor. The carpet at the window of the patio door just looked as if it was hacked,' she told the detectives.

However, she never saw any blood stains. Figuring that a forensic examination of the flat could only produce results, Mangan asked if the occupant would allow members of his team to examine the scene. If his suspicions were correct, he knew the flat at Richmond Cottages would contain traces of blood; if Noor had been killed here, it would have to.

In almost all cases where the victims of murder have been killed in a violent fashion, traces of important evidence are left behind. Mangan knew a murderer could dispose of a victim's body and mop up the blood, but without some heavy-duty cleaning chemicals, evidence would remain. Microscopic particles of blood left at the scene of a murder cling to most surfaces.

As a precautionary measure, Mangan sent a forensic team to the flat to take swabs from various locations in the room. If there were traces of blood, these could be matched against samples taken from the body parts, and Noor's son. These swabs were taken on 26 May.

Blood speckles are invisible to the naked eye, however, they can be seen if a chemical called luminal—a powdery compound made up of nitrogen, hydrogen, oxygen and carbon—is used to reveal their existence. Samples of the blood particles found at the scene were taken for comparison with those taken from the torso.

*****

Meanwhile, Kathleen continued to enquire about Noor's whereabouts in a desperate attempt to convince others that she thought he was alive. Her rationale was simple; if she knew he was dead, why would she have continued to search for him?

On 23 May, in what can only be described as a bizarre encounter, she approached Dermot Farrelly, a community Welfare Officer, who worked out of offices on Upper Gardiner Street. He later made a statement which read:

'Kathleen Mulhall came into the office and I spoke to her at the counter. She was by herself. She was worried about Farah Swaleh Noor. She didn't know his whereabouts. She was asking me to tell her from the records on file if we knew where Farah was, if we had any address for him. She wanted to know if we knew if he was alright. I told her that we weren't in a position to give out information to her. She then said that Farah might be using his real name. She said she didn't know how to spell the name but it was Sheila Swaleh, Shagu. That's how she pronounced the name.

'She wasn't clear on the exact pronunciation. I have put variations of the name into the system but there is no match that is similar to the name at all on our computer files.'

*****

The detective team had become deeply interested in their relationship. Working methodically, the team began to build a picture of the life they led. Kathleen was the victim of sustained and repeated violence at Noor's hands. This was later documented in her own statements but also in interviews from people who knew her. Why she continued to remain with him is open to conjecture.

The relationship between Noor and Kathleen was fraught with violence. Noor was a highly volatile and aggressive individual and this condition was exacerbated by his excessive drinking.

Reports prepared for the Director of Public Prosecutions on the case would later state that she was 'hospitalised on umpteen occasions as a result of beatings she received from the deceased.'

In fact, anyone who met the couple, even socially, couldn't help but notice the violence Noor dispensed on her. At one point, the team were even told that she may have given premature birth and lost a child as a result of a beating. However, gardaí found no evidence to support this allegation and Kathleen later denied that it ever happened.

In truth, the relationship went wrong from the start. The two had first met around 2002. It was an illicit one as Kathleen was still married. Regardless, she left the family home in Kilclare Gardens and moved to Cork with Noor, where they lived in rented accommodation in Glanmire.

Things went from bad to worse in Cork. Witnesses would later recall how Noor was always very abusive towards Kathleen, although one remarked that 'she could give as good as she got.'

Barry Sheehan, who came across the pair, would make a statement:

'He was extremely violent. When he was sober he was the nicest fella in the world, which wasn't often.'

On one occasion, according to Sheehan's statement, Kathleen told him that Noor had kicked the baby out of her—that she had been heavily pregnant.

Maureen Moran was the landlord of the accommodation where they stayed in Cork, although the couple only lived there for five weeks. While she was collecting rent one day, she noticed that Kathleen was covered in bruises. Kathleen told her that Noor had beaten her up.

They returned to Dublin in September 2004, and went to the Asylum Seekers Unit on Upper Gardiner Street for assistance.

At the time, they were interviewed by an official called Derek O'Connor who arranged accommodation for them at The Mountainview Bed and Breakfast in Tallaght.

Mary Andrews, the manager there, provided the accommodation. Their records show that Kathleen only remained there until 4 October. Andrews would later make a statement saying Noor was very violent towards Kathleen, that she said he was jealous and possessive, and that Kathleen wanted to leave him but was afraid he would find her wherever she went.

Noor, however, continued to live in the accommodation until 8 December.

Kathleen by this time had been housed in alternative hostel accommodation at Lismore House in Drumcondra, in the north inner city. The hostel was run by Hanji Bob with her husband Catalin Bob. On one occasion, she heard Kathleen and Farah arguing in Kathleen's bedroom. Bob stated that on that occasion, Noor referred to Kathleen as 'a fucking bitch.' However they remained a couple, and on 1 December, they moved into flat No. 1 at 17 Richmond Cottages. They remained there until Noor had vanished without trace.

Yet more evidence came the way of the team. This time it came from an entirely unexpected source. On 11 July, the incident room was secretly contacted by two members of the Mulhall family. It was John Mulhall Jnr and his brother James, who were in Wheatfield Prison. They wanted to speak to members of the team in private.

When they called, they stated they were in a position to supply information on the identity of the body. Not only this, but they said they could also name the perpetrators of the crime and identify the crime scene.

The team had managed to keep the developments secret. In order to authenticate the information the jailed brothers planned to reveal, they said nothing about the breakthroughs.

When they met the Mulhall brothers in the prison, the two named the victim as 'Farah', saying he was a former boyfriend of their mother, Kathleen. They went further, disclosing the scene of the killing as a flat at Richmond Cottages.

The detectives tasked with interrogating them remained silent in order to let them provide as much information as possible. The ploy worked. The secret contacts continued between the brothers and the team. The detectives asked the brothers to make a statement but both declined to do so. However, they continued to pass information.

*****

There is no doubt that Kathleen, Linda and Charlotte knew they were under suspicion. The actions of John Mulhall Snr suggest that he feared for his two daughters. Although it was never categorically proven, it appears that he may have returned to help the women dispose of the carpet removed from the flat at Richmond Cottages.

Meanwhile the investigation was now gathering momentum. While virtually everyone was sure that Noor had been the victim, it was confirmed days later on 15 July when the news came back that his DNA matched that of his son.

But there was more news. Dr Dorothy Ramsbottom of the Forensic Science Laboratory confirmed with 99% certainty that his DNA matched the blood samples found at Richmond Cottages; now they had a crime scene.

This was the news the team desperately wanted to hear. Mangan immediately arranged for a full technical examination of the flat at Richmond Cottages to be examined. This began on 21 July when a unit from the Garda Technical Bureau and the Forensic Science Laboratory began an inch by inch search of the flat, its fixtures and furniture. They were searching for evidence which could reveal how Noor died, particularly traces of blood. To find these, they used luminal powder with a liquid containing hydrogen peroxide. This was sprayed as a fine mist in the flat, after which all natural light was then screened off.

The test revealed tiny traces of blood at the base of a bunk bed in the bedroom. These emerged as a bluish-green light when an ultra violet light was shone. There was also blood-staining on other surfaces in the room, which indicated that someone had at least been assaulted in the bedroom. The low-down location of the blood indicated that he may even have been on the floor during the assault.

There was also evidence of blood-staining in the grooves of the pine planks of a wardrobe in the bedroom, but not on the surface of the planks. This was consistent with a clean-up taking place to remove blood-staining.

The team now had enough evidence to contemplate making arrests. They had four suspects in mind. John Snr, Kathleen, Linda and her sister Charlotte Mulhall.

CHAPTER FIVE

'Confession is the first step towards repentance.'

- *English proverb*

MATTERS HAD NOW reached a desperate stage for Linda and Charlotte. Linda could still not sleep at night and constantly broke down crying. Every time she closed her eyes, she saw Noor's face and the scene of his dismemberment. She would later remark that she could no longer look at a black person without wanting to cry. His face was etched in her consciousness.

She soon fell into a deep depression. At night, she would cry herself to sleep, imagining what the future held. She couldn't contemplate losing her children, whom she adored. The situation was worse for her because she felt she could talk to no one; she'd spent her life taking drugs and drinking in a desperate attempt to escape from reality. Now she wanted to do just that, but there was no way out. The more she thought about her choices, the more she realised she had none.

In her heart, she knew it was only a matter of time before the truth emerged.

Charlotte suffered similarly; she too was in the throes of depression. Her life had also fallen apart. Like Linda, she drank at every opportunity to block out the memories of what had happened. Though they did not dare admit it to themselves; they woke each morning with a sense of dread and foreboding; this dread affected their every waking moment.

In their hearts, they knew that once the body had been found and positively identified, it was only a matter of time before the Gardaí would come. The waiting for the inevitable to happen, more than anything else, was like torture.

However, the premonitions of an imminent arrest were correct. The statement Bakaar and Hyland had made had specifically named them as being amongst the last to see Noor alive. When they were named, the inquiry team had discreetly run every conceivable background check on the two.

Mangan had studied the information, paying attention to the details, and the women's personal history. He didn't need a fortune teller to reveal the murder was no ordinary one. When he examined the paperwork on the women, which detailed their history, it was clear to him that the death probably hadn't been planned, or even premeditated. This analysis created more questions than answers though. The primary question being: what had happened?

The matter was further complicated by secret evidence the team obtained from Crime and Security, the spying department of Garda Headquarters. As part of their investigation, Mangan had asked for officials in the security department to analyse all calls made to and from the suspects' mobile phones. The examination of these showed that John Mulhall Snr had been in touch with his daughters at the time Noor was killed, certainly in the hours after it. This also made him a suspect, though it appeared that he had visited the scene and fled when he had seen what happened.

Mangan was of the opinion that the inquiry should now proceed as carefully as possible; experience had shown him that investigations like this were best carried out in a deliberately slow and methodical manner.

He directed the team to first try talk to the women, and then, and only then, move to make arrests. This line of inquiry was tried but rejected. When the detective team spoke to the sisters and their father John, it proved fruitless. The answers Kathleen gave to enquiries made of her did not seem to tie up with what gardaí suspected. With no place left to turn, Mangan sought permission to make arrests.

These took place on 3 August. On that particular morning, the team gathered in Fitzgibbon Street Station for a conference addressed by Mangan. The instructions were as follows:

Linda, Charlotte, Kathleen and John Mulhall Snr were to be arrested under Section 4 of the Criminal Law Act 1997, for murder. The arresting team was given the exact locations where the four could be found. In the days prior to the arrests, Mangan had briefed members of several teams who would be tasked with interrogating the suspects. Much preparation work and planning had been done in this regard. Convinced that the moment for arrests had come, Mangan was adamant that everything should go according to plan.

In an address to the conference, he outlined the facts that had been established. All knew full well that the interrogation of a suspect was the most important part of any investigation. Interrogators must watch an interviewee like a hawk. If a suspect shows the slightest sign of confessing, it must be seized upon.

The plan he drafted was simple. They would have on average two hours to interview each suspect before they were entitled to take a break.

Each team would ask simple questions and try pressurising each individual suspect into telling the truth, or confessing what they knew.

The team could prove that Noor had been killed, and probably dismembered, in the flat at Richmond Cottages. They also knew Charlotte, Linda and Kathleen had been with him on the day he died.

Once they confirmed they had been with him, the team would then confront each suspect with a series of facts. What followed would largely depend on the answers they received. The purpose of the interview, though, would be to establish the truth, specifically who had done what.

Linda was the first to be arrested—at her home in Kilclare Gardens shortly after 10am, by Detective Sergeant Walter O'Connell from Store Street. This was almost five months after Noor's death.

The timing of the arrest ensured it was done without any unnecessary drama. More than anything, Mangan didn't want her children to see her being taken away.

O'Connell was one of the city's most experienced officers. When he called to her door, he was polite and told her the purpose of his call. Linda was visibly stunned, although she had been waiting for this day for some time. Now it had finally arrived, she didn't know what to say or how to react. Like an actor in a film, who had rehearsed her part 1,000 times, the drama of the situation didn't outwardly affect her. She had rehearsed it so many times in her mind that it had no effect. She was taken to Store Street Station.

Charlotte was simultaneously arrested at another location in Tallaght, by Detective Sergeant Liam Hickey. He was one of the few detectives who had been updated on every aspect of the investigation.

Charlotte looked shocked when she was approached. She said nothing. Her body language gave nothing away. She was taken by car to Mountjoy Garda Station for her interrogation.

Kathleen had been walking along Summerhill Parade, not far from the canal, when an unmarked patrol car pulled up. She had moved into a small flat close to Richmond Cottages.

Two detectives, one of whom was Detective Sergeant Gerry McDonnell, stepped out of the vehicle, and formally arrested her on the street. She didn't put up a fight and readily sat into the car. She was then driven to Mountjoy Station.

The sisters' father John was arrested in south Dublin, in the grounds of Terenure College, by David O'Brien, a detective who had worked on the inquiry since the beginning, and Adrian Murray. Of the four arrests, his would prove to be the most proverbial.

Before the arrest teams left the station, Mangan had asked O'Brien and Murray to arrest Mulhall without too much fuss. He was conscious of disturbing children in the school, but he also figured that Mulhall had covered for his two daughters out of pure love.

The team knew he hadn't been present when Noor was killed, having examined the phone traffic between the suspects, hence it was logical to surmise that his involvement had been to protect his daughters. Given the circumstances, they felt it safe to assume he had no interest in helping Kathleen, if she had a case to answer.

On the morning of the arrest, Mulhall went into shock when he saw the detectives approach.

He had been fitting glass windows at the school and had anticipated an arrest at home. He made no effort to resist but asked O'Brien for one thing; he wanted to smoke a cigarette before he was taken away. There is no doubt that he didn't expect his request to be granted. To his surprise, O'Brien told him to take as much time as he needed.

This act of kindness had a profound affect on Mulhall whose life was falling apart. Whether it was the circumstances he was facing at that moment in time, or something else, the gesture struck him as a magnanimous one. When he smoked his cigarette, he gathered his thoughts and then sat into the patrol car. He was then taken into the city centre, where his interrogation began.

News of the arrests spread like wildfire. His daughter, Marie, was in work at the time, when a neighbour called to say Linda and Charlotte had been arrested.

She would later make a statement saying: 'I returned from work and met the Gardaí at the house. My sisters, Linda and Charlotte, had been arrested at that stage and were gone to a Garda Station. I tried to ring my father but could not get him.'

He was now in custody. She could do nothing but wait and see what happened. Thoughtful as ever, she collected Linda's children and looked after them for the day.

Meanwhile, the teams of detectives spent hours interviewing each of the suspects. None of them uttered a word of any importance; instead they sometimes retained their right to silence, or gave varying accounts of their movements.

The common denominator was a full denial of any role in the killing. Kathleen maintained that Noor was still alive somewhere, and said she had been trying to locate him. She could even give the names of several people whom she had asked.

The four were released without charge 12 hours later. While some interpreted this as the possible end of the investigation; the arrests were in fact just the beginning.

*****

The arrests had caused the four to panic, but they had a knock-on effect on the entire Mulhall family, including Marie. She had travelled to Store Street Garda Station around 11pm to meet her father, John, with her extended family. They took John Snr, Linda and Charlotte home while Kathleen looked after herself. Later that night, according to her statement, she spoke to her father.

'There was just myself and my father, John, there. I asked him why he was arrested. He told me that the police think he moved the body of

Farah Noor after he was killed. He told me he had nothing to do with moving the body, nor had he anything to do with the killing of Farah Noor.

'He assured me he did not do anything that would have got him into trouble and I took him at his word. I told him the story that Charlotte told me in the bathroom and he appeared to know what had actually happened,' she later said.

While Linda had been terrified at first when she was arrested, she interpreted her release from custody as a sign that there was no evidence against her. Her release somewhat restored her confidence.

Marie, at the time, was not talking to Linda. She was frightened for her father, to whom she was close. But she did sense Linda's new-found confidence.

In her statement she said: 'I think Linda Mulhall though that the killing of Farah was finished with when she was released. She was sure she got away with it. I never discussed the story Charlotte had told me in the bathroom with her following her arrest.'

However, Linda's confidence would not last for long.

*****

The team continued to gather as much evidence as possible, with the intention of pressing charges. No stone was left unturned. On 14 August, they became aware that John Mulhall Snr had dumped bags in the Liffey at Leixlip. Mangan arranged for a search team to go straight to the area where a green plastic refuse bin, blanket, duvet, duvet cover, and pillow were found. There was also a bag that contained hair, and a knife with a black handle. It later transpired, however, that this was completely unrelated to Noor's killing.

News of this particular search quickly filtered back to the suspects, as Mangan's team had also searched a house in the area. This belonged to an innocent associate of John Mulhall's who often gave him work.

Marie, by this stage, had had enough. She could see her father's life being destroyed before her eyes.

'I tackled my sister, Linda, in the house. Linda was living in the house at the time. I could see that loads of people that had nothing to do with the killing of Farah Noor were being dragged into Farah's death. I told Linda Mulhall that if she did not go and tell the Garda what she knew, I would tell them the story Charlotte Mulhall had told me about Farah Noor's killing,' she later said in a statement.

The decision by Mangan to treat the four with more respect than perhaps they deserved had been fortuitous. Although the sisters had remained mostly silent and certainly not co-operative while in custody, Mangan sincerely believed the women, Linda more than the others, were certainly traumatised by what had happened. His opinion was shared by those familiar with the evidence that had been assembled so far. This view also applied to the sisters' father, John.

Everyone on the team sensed he was desperately upset and more than anything, wanted to protect his daughters, no matter what they'd done.

This analysis was the correct one. He had been overcome by the events of the previous five months. He suffered from contrasting emotions; he could not understand how his daughters had dismembered a body. No matter what way he examined their actions; it made no sense to him.

He had been left devastated by Kathleen's decision to end their marriage. Now the man who'd taken his wife had died, and would take two of his daughters as well. No one could understand the position that he found himself in. O'Brien's act of generosity on the morning of his arrest in some ways restored Mulhall's faith. He had never had much time for the police; now he saw them in a different light. While he was no pushover, he was privately appalled by what had happened to Noor. No matter what way he examined his conscience, he felt he had only one choice, and that was to tell the truth.

He spent several days and nights trying to work out what to do or say. In the midst of the turmoil, he focused his thoughts and decided to do what he believed was right. His was not an easy decision to make.

On the morning of 17 August, he called the incident room and asked for Liam Hickey, the Detective Sergeant who always seemed to be in the centre of things.

Mulhall said he wanted to talk. This was an unexpected move. Hickey wasted no time in arranging to meet, and called Mangan within minutes of the call ending, to alert him. The two detectives interpreted the contact as a good omen. Their analysis proved correct.

Mulhall had wanted to meet somewhere discreet, and suggested a side street off Cork Street around 11.30am that same morning. When he arrived, he shook their hands; he was not hostile. In fact, Mangan sensed he was nervous and agitated.

Tradecraft had taught the two detectives to remain silent at times like this. They both knew

Mulhall was in a no-win situation and was trying to do the right thing, though it was clear he wanted to make sure he wouldn't be charged as an accessory. Eventually he began to speak.

He spoke in a low voice at first. Linda, he said, knew where Noor's head was hidden. He continued to speak, all the time struggling to say the words. He urged Mangan to talk to his eldest daughter personally. He said he knew his daughter; that she was a good woman, and was sure she would tell the truth. Linda, he said, was terrified, and he was afraid for her. His analysis seemed reasonable, certainly from a father's point of view.

The meeting lasted no more than ten minutes. Mangan said he understood the situation, and promised to call to the family home later that night. He gave Mulhall his word and they shook hands.

That night, Mangan and Hickey drove to the Mulhall home in Kilclare Gardens in Tallaght. They were greeted by Mulhall Snr, who was waiting to meet them when they arrived. He invited the detectives into his home, offered them some tea, and asked them to sit in the front room.

He explained that Linda wasn't there yet but was on her way home. He said she had just collected her social welfare from Kevin Street and was delayed. They waited for almost two hours but Linda didn't return home. Mulhall tried to reach her on her mobile phone but it was turned off. Eventually Mangan said it was best that they leave, though he promised to call back in the morning. This was a setback, but he didn't give up hope. Instead he left his mobile phone switched on, should Linda return.

Later that night, Mulhall Snr called; he sounded distraught. He said Linda had been admitted to hospital. She had tried to cut her wrists while in the throes of a depression.

Mangan asked if she was okay, adding that his team was there to help if there was anything they could do. This was a sincere offer. Her father thanked him for his kindness once more.

*****

It was clear that Linda was not an unrepentant killer, but she had not made the decision to confess. No one on the team believed Charlotte to be a calculated murderer either. Although some possessed doubts about their father's motives, he was largely considered an honest man caught up in a calamitous and horrible scenario. Life for him was slowly descending into a nightmare and this was compounded by Linda's self harm. This is why the team waited two days before attempting to reopen their discussions, though it is noteworthy that the team were taking him on face value.

Hickey was tasked with making the call to him and arranging to call once again to the house—providing that Linda was well enough to accept a visit.

Mulhall asked them to come at once.

However, when they arrived at the house at 11.15am that same morning; she refused to talk. The detectives could not even make eye contact with her; she sat in the corner staring at the ground; looking inconsolable.

Mangan attempted to speak but she would not respond. All she would say was that she knew nothing about Farah.

She denied all knowledge of what had happened to Noor. She was her old self again, or so they suspected. Both Mangan and Hickey knew she was lying, but not in a conventional sense; they felt she was deeply troubled, her mind in turmoil. It was plain to see. She looked as if she had not slept in days.

Mangan made some small talk for about 20 minutes. He then asked her about the injuries on her arms. For some reason, the comment took Linda by surprise. Slowly she began to open up. Awkwardly, she explained that she had cut herself.

Mangan sympathised, telling her that she was helping no one by hurting herself, and that she needed to look after herself.

Hickey agreed with the sentiments and the two of them urged her to tell the truth. Linda, though, wasn't ready. Exasperated, Mangan said he would do whatever he could to help, but told her that the inquiry was not going to go away.

He spoke directly and honestly to her. He said he believed she knew where Noor's head was buried. Linda made a half-hearted attempt at denying the allegation, but not even she believed her own words.

Finally, when he had said all he could, Mangan proclaimed the inquiry would continue until he found out what had happened.

Linda didn't interpret this as a threat, as it wasn't. In her heart, she understood that it was just a statement of fact.

John Mulhall Snr had said nothing during the conversation. He now brought in tea, which relaxed the atmosphere.

Towards the end of the informal meeting, Mangan mentioned that her brothers John Jnr and James had contacted the incident room, and said he would be speaking to other members of the family. This took Linda by surprise temporarily, but she didn't break down. Once again, she said she couldn't help.

The detectives had now exhausted every avenue with her. Neither Mangan nor Hickey reacted to her denials, which they knew were lies. Having tried everything, Mangan asked if he could speak to her father alone. Linda then left the room.

John Mulhall Snr returned moments later. He asked the two officers if she had confessed to anything, or had even been helpful, only to be told that she hadn't. He seemed genuinely disappointed. He shook his head, and said he knew that she knew where it was, referring to Noor's missing head.

Privately, Mangan resigned himself to the fact that this was not going to be easy. He thanked Mulhall for his help, and told him he'd done what he could.

At that moment, the father's mobile rang. It was his daughter, Marie. He spoke quietly to her for a few minutes, and when he finished, he said Marie wished to make a statement that Saturday if possible, as Charlotte had spoken to her about Noor's death.

Mangan thanked him for his help and said he understood. He didn't need to say any more.

Rather than leave Linda on bad terms, the detective made a point of thanking her for her time and said he hoped her injuries would heal. He then shook her hand.

Mangan and Hickey left the house not really knowing their next move. The two drove back into the city, and wondered about Linda. Privately they both feared she would hurt herself again, as she appeared to be deeply depressed.

The investigation was once more helped by Marie, who had done the right thing from the start. At all times, she had told her father and two sisters to tell the truth, if not for themselves, for their loved ones. She no longer spoke to her mother, so she had no influence there.

On that night, she and Linda argued. According to her statement:

'Myself and Linda Mulhall had a blazing row. Linda Mulhall seemed to think that she was in the clear. I then told my father, John, who was present during this row that if Linda Mulhall did not tell the police what she knew I was leaving. I then left the house. A short time later my father rang me on my mobile and told me that he was going to ring the police and get them to come to Linda and she was going to tell them everything.'

*****

Mangan was called to a meeting in Coolock. Moments after he arrived on the north side of Dublin city, his phone rang. It was Linda; she was crying and was barely comprehensible.

'Christopher, Christopher, I need to talk to you.'

Mangan was taken aback. He asked if she wished to talk about the murder. She said she did. He told her he would call around to the house at 4.45pm that same evening.

He returned as promised with Hickey. As before, John Mulhall Snr met them at the door. He directed them to a bedroom that was built in the back garden of the house. When they entered the room, they saw Linda sitting on the bed. She was crying uncontrollably. Mangan walked towards her and asked if she wanted her father to stay, but she said she'd prefer to talk alone.

Perhaps for the first time in months, she felt relieved. Wiping away the tears, she admitted that she, with Charlotte, had killed Noor.

Mangan was legally obliged at this stage to caution her and ask her to make a statement. He explained that he was duty bound to do so. She accepted his words as sincere and said she just wanted to tell the truth.

Hickey then cautioned her in a standard

manner:

'You are not obliged to say anything unless you wish to do so, but anything you do say will be taken down and may be given in evidence.'

He took out his notebook while asking her if she understood the caution. He then proceeded to write down what was the beginning of Linda's confession, word for word. She continued to cry uncontrollably as she spoke about the events of 20 March.

It was clear that she had been deeply traumatised by what had happened; perhaps horrified by her own actions. She had now accepted that she could not brazen this out.

Mangan offered to take her to Tallaght Garda Station to record her interview, but she declined.

She wanted to confess there.

'I want to tell you the truth about what happened Farah,' she said.

She recalled the events of that afternoon and specifically how the atmosphere in Richmond Cottages had suddenly turned. She spoke honestly, not hiding anything, and then asked if she could use the toilet, at 6pm. When she returned, she spoke about the actual killing.

She didn't attempt to limit her own involvement in the death. She broke down crying several times, while confessing, and spoke about the effects of the dismemberment.

When she finished, Hickey read over the notes of the conversation, which he crafted into a statement. She agreed with the notes and signed them. The time was now 8pm.

That evening was bright, prompting Mangan to ask Linda if she would take him to the field where she had buried the head. She agreed to do this without hesitation. Mangan left the room momentarily to tell her father what had happened; he seemed relieved. The detectives then left with Linda in a patrol car.

Linda directed them out of the estate and towards Killinarden Hill, where she'd hidden Noor's head in a field.

Hickey parked the patrol car on a grass verge adjacent to the field. Mangan and Linda stepped out of the car and walked towards the area. The entrance to the field was covered with rubbish and protected by barbed wire. Mangan held the barbed wire down while Linda stepped across.

The two then walked down the field. While they walked, she pointed at a burned out car she recalled seeing previously. She directed Mangan to a clearing near some bushes at the entrance to the ditch; she then got down on her hunkers.

She pointed towards a cement pipe in the ditch and said she had smashed the head and thrown it into a stream. This was what she thought she remembered doing with it, but it must have been hard for her to remember exactly, considering the amount of alcohol she had consumed that night. Mangan could do no more. He helped her out of the ditch and they walked back to the car.

As they did so, Mangan asked if she would go to Tallaght Garda Station to have her statement read over to her on video; he was leaving nothing to chance. While his instincts told him Linda was being honest, experience had taught him that she could change her mind just as easily.

However, Linda volunteered to help him without hesitation. They arrived at Tallaght Station at 9.15pm. Mick Leahy was the Duty Sergeant in charge that night, and he booked them into an interview room.

Inside the room, Mangan explained once more that he wanted to record her statement being read out to her on video. He then cautioned her.

Hickey then began writing out the statement again. Leahy had explained to Linda that she was not under arrest and could leave at any time. She said she understood.

Hickey then read out the statement she had made in her home, this time recording it for the record.

Linda didn't waiver. She agreed with everything and identified that it was her signature on the statement he'd taken earlier. During this interview, she once again broke down crying several times. Privately, Mangan and Hickey couldn't help but be moved by her distress; she was inconsolable. The more she talked about the actual killing and dismemberment, the more she cried; though she insisted that she wanted to get the interview over with. In some ways, they felt she was expunging the memories of the killing through confessing.

Once the notes were read over to her and the paperwork was in order, the two detectives took her home.

On the journey back to Kilclare Gardens, Mangan asked if she would point out the locations where she had first hidden the head and discarded the knives used in the dismemberment. Although she was tired, the park was on their way home, so she agreed.

This took no more than a few minutes.

When they arrived at Kilclare Gardens later that night, John Mulhall Snr was there waiting at the front door.

He greeted Mangan with a handshake; then hugged his daughter. He looked as if he were about to cry.

Linda was also very emotional and hugged both Mangan and Hickey. She thanked them for understanding and said sorry for all the trouble she had caused. She broke down once more.

She stood motionless in the front garden as the two detectives returned to the car. Moments before he left, Mangan told her she had done the right thing, and asked her to get some sleep.

The detectives were seen leaving the house by Marie that same night.

'I spoke to her [Linda] and asked her if she had told the story. She told me she had told them everything. She explained to me about Farah's head. She told me she had moved the head from Tymon Park North to Killinarden Park. She told me that all three of them, herself, Charlotte and Kathleen Mulhall, had buried the head, but she had moved it herself to Killinarden Park. I told her to tell the story of Farah Noor's death to the Garda so that my father would left alone,' she said in her statement.

She only ever wanted to protect her father, who had told her that he had not been involved. She repeated this denial to gardaí in her own statements.

'My father kept saying he had nothing to do with Farah's death,' she said.

From that moment on, she never discussed Noor's death with Linda. Nor did she raise it with Charlotte.

'I did not want to know,' she later explained to gardaí.

The two detectives left Tallaght that night at 10.15pm and headed back to Fitzgibbon Street Garda Station to write up a record of what had happened. They alerted their own superiors to the developments and worked late into the night on their respective files before heading home. Linda's confession was not the end of the case; it was only the beginning.

Chapter Six

'Always tell the truth. That way, you don't have to remember what you said.'

- Mark Twain

THE INTERROGATION OF Linda Mulhall didn't end with the confession. Although she had made a statement admitting her role in the killing, and co-operated as best she could, Mangan was legally obliged to follow up every line of inquiry. Foremost in his mind was the urgent need to locate the victim's head, which was still missing. It was imperative that every effort be made to locate it as fast as possible for humane as much as evidential reasons.

The following morning, 20 August, he returned

to Kilclare Gardens, accompanied once more by Hickey. They arrived in Tallaght about 11.20am.

Linda had been expecting their arrival and was waiting at the door. She invited them into the sitting room of the house. She looked apprehensive but more rested; she'd slept for the first time in months.

Mangan thanked her for being honest. He said he knew how difficult it must have been for her to confess, but assured her she had made the correct decision. He then explained that he would need her help to identify where she had buried the head. This had to be found.

The inspector was careful to explain that from now on, all his dealing would be formal. In other words, he would have to administer a legal caution to her. He proceeded to do so and she said she understood.

The two detectives knew Linda's statements would eventually result in her being charged; therefore they made a point of constantly reminding her that she didn't have to assist them in the inquiry. Linda, though, insisted she wanted to. Later that morning, she was taken to the Sean Walsh Memorial Park, off the Old Bawn Road. This was the location, she told gardaí in her statement, where she, Charlotte and her mother had buried Noor's head and disposed of the knives.

The park itself is overlooked by the Dublin Mountains, and contains formal gardens with water features including ponds and waterfalls.

She directed the two detectives to one of the gardens opposite the Plaza Hotel. Her recollection of where she had hidden the evidence was clear. She directed them straight to a lake where she said the hammer and knives had been thrown. She then pointed to an area behind a park bench where she said Charlotte had dug a hole with a knife and buried the head.

The team had to treat each location as a crime scene. In this regard, Mangan had requested that other members of the team meet at the park to cordon it off.

These pieces of information, which effectively corroborated her story, were crucial to solving the case. Her help permitted the team to retrieve the knives and hammer used in the attack and dismemberment. Because of her willingness to co-operate, the team was able to build a detailed picture of the sequence of events as they had unfolded; certainly to the best of her recollection.

She left the park at noon accompanied by Mangan and Hickey, and next drove to a housing estate off the Tallaght by-pass. Once again, she showed a willingness to do whatever was necessary to assist the team, even though it was to her own detriment. While Hickey parked the patrol car, Linda took Mangan into Killinarden Estate.

She now retraced her footsteps. As she walked, she spoke to Mangan about what she had done. Mangan had been joined by Detective Sergeant Colm Fox, who coincidentally had been one of the first gardaí on the scene when Noor's body was found.

Killinarden is a predominantly working class estate, which has suffered from social exclusion since it was built. Walking through the concrete jungle, Linda explained why she had taken the head from its original resting place. At the time, it made perfect sense; she was afraid someone would find it.

Fox listened attentively to the killer as she dictated what had happened, pointing out certain areas. When she finished, Mangan asked him to preserve the scene; they then returned to the car.

It would be incorrect to assume that Linda had enabled the inquiry team to break the case though. The information provided by Bakaar had done that, but she did reveal the specifics and most importantly why Noor had died. While it is conceivable that the Director of Public Prosecutions would have pressed charges on the basis of the forensic evidence obtained from Richmond Cottages; the reason behind the killing and why Noor had been dismembered would have remained a mystery.

Linda's decision to come clean, more than anything else, gave the inquiry team the valuable information they required to pursue every aspect of the case. However, there is no doubt that she confessed because she could no longer live with the guilt. In some ways, she saw her co-operation with the team as an exercise in cleansing her guilt; she was doing the right thing by Noor, even though it would have calamitous consequences for her.

When she had finished clarifying the few remaining questions that were outstanding, she asked to be brought home. She was physically and mentally exhausted.

She wanted to be with her children. She planned to cook them a special dinner, she said, and make them a trifle. The remark struck many of the team as unusual, given the circumstances, though it reinforced the notion that she was a vulnerable woman.

The truth was that Mangan had enough information and crime scenes to search and examine. But he did ask if she could meet the next morning to clarify other outstanding matters, which had presented themselves. Linda, once again, agreed to meet without hesitation, though, there was purpose in the request from Mangan.

He had a residual fear that she would change her mind, deny what she had said, and claim to have been coerced into confessing. He was experienced enough to know this was a distinct possibility and one that couldn't be ruled out.

This partly explains why he proceeded to gather as many statements and as much evidence as was humanly possible.

The search of the lake in the Sean Walsh Memorial Park located the weapons that Linda had said were used to kill Noor. However, there was still no sign of the missing head. The search of the hillside where Linda had secretly buried it had revealed nothing. Mangan knew she wasn't lying, which led the team to conclude it must have been moved elsewhere by a dog, or wildlife. There was no doubt this was a setback.

*****

Regardless, Mangan and Hickey returned to Kilclare Gardens the next morning, arriving there at 11.50am. This time, the door was answered by one of Linda's children. They were polite and mannerly, and asked the detectives to go into the sitting room and take a seat.

As they waited, John Mulhall Snr came into the room. He shook their hands before offering tea and biscuits once again. He then left the room and called Linda downstairs.

She looked flustered. She apologised for leaving them waiting. As was now procedure, she accompanied them to the station where she was cautioned. Mangan informed the Duty Sergeant that she was there of her own free will and had volunteered to be interviewed. Linda confirmed this was the case. The three were then shown to an interview room. Hickey inserted an audio tape into a recorder and administered a legal caution. They once again told her she was free to leave at any time, for the benefit of the tape.

This interview was conducted with the intention of corroborating the information she had provided with the items retrieved from the park the day before.

Mangan began by explaining that he wanted to ask her specific questions about the scenes they had visited. He also explained that he wanted to drive her into the city, where she could identify specific locations while being filmed. This would confirm the facts she'd already disclosed. Linda, once again, said, 'That's grand.'

That interview began with a series of straight questions.

'In your statement, you referred to Charlie. Is that your sister Charlotte?'

'Yes.'

The questions that followed were simple but they had a purpose. They showed Linda reaffirming what she had earlier said. If an allegation was to be raised at a later date in a trial situation, the team would be able to show that Linda had confessed to the crime over a number of days, and reaffirmed her story.

'You mentioned that you had ecstasy with you. How many did you have?

'About ten.'

'How many did you take?

'I know I said one, but when I went back home there was none left. I do know me mam only crushed up one, and put it into Farah's drink.'

'Were they a particular type of E.'

'I think they were butterflies,' she added.

The interview continued.

The detectives took her through her story once more; they went over the actual murder and the events that preceded it.

The interrogation was difficult for Linda in many ways. She constantly cried, forcing the detectives to stop certain lines of questioning; though every time, she insisted on continuing.

An important part of this interview was her absolute denial that her father had been involved in the killing.

In the interview, she denied categorically that she told him about the killing, or what had transpired. She said he hadn't known about anything.

'Did you ever tell your dad?' the detectives asked.

'No.'

'Your dad had no part in this?' they asked again.

'No.'

This could not have been true, as he had visited the flat hours after the killing.

They also asked about the dismemberment and disposal of the body. Linda said she couldn't remember the specifics; she was telling the truth.

'How long did it take? Hours?' asked Mangan.

'No I don't know. I remember some things. I remember about the bag.'

'How long would it have taken for you to go to the canal with the parts?'

'About six times.'

The detectives needed specifics; so they encouraged Linda to tell them as much as possible, even to give them information that she saw as irrelevant. They asked more questions about the weight of the bags, and the route taken from the flat to the canal, to ensure she was telling the truth.

Emotional and tearful, she explained the sequence of events; how she had walked from her mother's flat, on to Main Road, and to the canal. She withheld nothing.

The focus of the interview then changed. The detectives concentrated on showing that Linda must have been involved in the killing, as she knew the details. This again was aimed at revealing her knowledge of the killing to make sure she was not accepting responsibility for a crime she didn't commit, or possibly trying to protect others.

'As regards clothes, we found jeans in the canal. Was he wearing jeans?' they asked.

'Don't know,' she answered.

'Underpants. Was he wearing ones that night?' was the next question.

'Yes.'

'Any reason why they were left on him?' they asked.

'I don't know.'

'He had jewellery. Where did it go?' they asked.

'Charlotte sold it or gave it away.'

The detectives were particularly keen to know who knew what. Had she discussed the killing with anyone? This was of vital importance.

'After he was killed, did you meet and discuss it many times?'

'Not really. We did not even talk about it. I could see the way Ma and Charlotte had changed; they could see how I had changed.'

She broke down once again. At this point, Mangan offered to terminate the interview. She was now crying uncontrollably and couldn't be consoled. More than anything, the gardaí didn't want to be seen to have pressurised her into saying anything or making a confession. This became a common theme in their dealing, though, in fairness, Linda never held back any information.

She continued to dictate her story. She next spoke about plans she had fermented in her mind if she were to be charged. She had spoken to her brother James, not about the killing, but about who would care for her children should something happen to her.

'When I say I talked to James, I asked him to look after the kids if anything happened,' she told them. The day's interview concluded on that note.

As they left the interview room, she asked to be taken to a toilet. It was now 1.55pm in the afternoon. Mangan was now armed with more hard information. As they left, he told Sergeant Duncan Byrne they were leaving Tallaght Station to point out scenes.

As they drove to Fitzgibbon Street, Linda asked could they stop and get coffee. She had a splitting headache. Retelling the story affected her greatly.

Mangan drove on to the station but brought her to the station's kitchen when they arrived. There, Linda made coffee for them all and smoked a cigarette. Her mind was in turmoil now. She kept having flashbacks; she replayed the killing over and over again.

They left the station an hour later in a patrol car. As they drove through the north inner city, Linda said she recognised the Sunset House Pub and directed Hickey to turn left and left again ,and then right into Richmond Cottages.

She then pointed out No. 17.

Mangan then asked her to step out of the car and point out the flat where she had killed Noor.

The front door was locked but Mangan rang the bell and one of the other tenants answered. She then walked into the hall and pointed out Flat No. 1. It was the first time she had been to the flat since the killing.

As she did this, she broke down crying; she was uncontrollable. She could not look anyone in the face. Instead she just cried and cried. Returning to the scene of the killing was too much. Mangan asked if she wanted to go home; she said yes without hesitation. He took her straight home.

The offer did not have the calming affect the detectives had hoped for.

During the 40 minute drive to Tallaght, Linda cried, this time hysterically. She said she'd always been in the wrong place at the wrong time. She spoke about how Noor had beaten her mother up too. She also spoke about self harm and how she couldn't get Noor's face out of her mind. She was a troubled woman.

There was nothing the detectives could do; they could offer her no solace as they both knew she would most likely be charged. Instead they allowed her to speak.

They arrived back at the Mulhall house at 3.30pm. Mangan walked her back into the house.

When Linda saw her father, she hugged him and kissed him, almost leaning on him.

John Mulhall Snr thanked the gardaí, and Mangan told Linda to call him on his mobile if she needed anything. She said that she'd help him further if he needed things clarified. She hugged him and thanked him for his kindness.

That afternoon was a difficult one. Mangan figured Linda wasn't a ruthless killer, yet she had committed a ruthless crime. However, he couldn't ignore the emotional turmoil she appeared to be in. He had never dealt with a killer like this before. There were still lingering doubts over the involvement of her father.

When they left the house, the two detectives went straight to Killinarden Hill, which was now being searched. The search teams had found nothing. When he was informed of the news, the two went back to the incident room.

*****

While the gardaí continued to forensically examine the crime scenes, they didn't approach Linda again until 2 September. There was no point. They had, by this stage, retrieved what they could find from the Royal Canal and the park in Tallaght, but they could still not recover Noor's head. They knew Linda hadn't lied when she said she had disposed of the head in Killinarden but it just wasn't there anymore.

Accompanied once again by Hickey, Mangan called to see Linda at her home. They found her in an advanced state of depression. She looked unwell; in fact; she looked shattered. She was a broken woman.

This analysis was confirmed when she told the gardaí she was having difficultly sleeping, although she felt better having confessed. She asked if her mother and Charlotte had talked to the gardaí yet, but showed no reaction when she heard they hadn't.

The purpose of Mangan's visit was to ensure he had as much evidence as possible to press charges against her, though in essence he wished to establish specifically who had done what. This would allow him to bring charges against Charlotte, Kathleen and anyone else involved.

In this regard, he wanted her once again to point out the various crime scenes, and to retrace the route they had taken in the city centre. Linda agreed to this but said she couldn't do it right then as she had no babysitter, but that she would gladly do it another day.

Before Mangan left he advised her to see her doctor about getting sleeping pills to help her. Both gardaí were struck by Linda's appearance, which seemed to be deteriorating rapidly.

When Hickey and Mangan next returned to Kilclare Gardens, they found Linda in the kitchen ironing. She looked slightly better. As they had a cup of coffee, she revealed that Charlotte had told her that she planned on turning herself in. He had heard all of this before.

Mangan didn't pass any remark on this, but asked Linda if she could now go with them to clarify some things in relation to the crime scenes. He explained that this would be video recorded. She readily agreed, and once she had been officially cautioned, they headed off towards Killinarden Hill.

There they met Detective Garda Dominic Cox, who Mangan explained would record her on film. The four walked into the field where Linda said she had buried Noor's head. She pointed out the same place as she had previously shown him. Furthermore she said that she was certain she was in the right place. Although they hadn't found Noor's skull, Mangan figured she was telling the truth; there was no reason for her not to.

The next place they visited was the boardwalk in central Dublin, where she had taken drugs before the killing. Linda was unemotional as she showed the gardaí which bench they had sat on as they drank vodka and consumed the ecstasy tablets.

She then retraced her steps until they drove to Ballybough Bridge.

From a distance, Linda confirmed that it was the bridge where they had dumped the body parts.

She then became very distressed and said that she could not go back under the bridge, or back into the flat at Richmond Cottages. Tears once again streamed from her eyes. She wept uncontrollably.

It took a few minutes for her to calm down and the gardaí gave her time to compose herself. It was no use. It was clear to all that she couldn't contemplate approaching the actual scene of the killing because they brought back too many demons and nightmares.

Instead they went to Mountjoy Garda Station so they could show her the exhibits.

This relaxed her somewhat. On arrival in the station, Linda appeared quiet and asked for some coffee. As she sipped her coffee she was reminded that she wasn't under arrest and she could leave at any time, but she said she wanted to stay and continue yet again.

They interviewed her for a few hours, and once again Linda became very emotional as she recalled what she had done to Noor. It was clear that she found it difficult to talk about the actual death, but she found some sort of peace in continuing to confess. This is perhaps why she always declined to take a break in garda custody and continued making her confession.

Soon after she finished the interview, Charlotte rang her on her mobile phone. When she heard Linda was with the gardaí, Charlotte told her that she also was going to talk to them.

CHAPTER SEVEN

'It is easier to talk than to hold one's tongue.'

- Greek Proverb

THE NEWS THAT Noor's true name was Sheilila Salim, and that he was Kenyan, advanced the investigation. As a consequence, renewed efforts were made in the attempt to locate the victim's family. This task was given to Gerry McDonnell, one of the detectives who had immersed himself in the inquiry.

When he received the news that Noor was not who he claimed to be; he once again dedicated himself to tracing the victim's friends and family.

The detective sergeant liaised with Garda

Headquarters, who in turn contacted Interpol, the international police agency. The actual process of locating the family was fraught with bureaucracy and took weeks. Though, eventually on 12 September, McDonnell received the news that his counterparts in Mombassa had spoken to a woman who they believed was Noor's wife. Her name was Husna Mohamed Said. She had already been informed of the death.

Although Noor had abandoned her years before, leaving her to care for a young family; she was shocked and horrified when she was told what had become of him. Like Kathleen, Noor had brutalised her and abandoned his children for a life in Europe.

She answered McDonnell's questions as best she could, and promised to do what she could to help. McDonnell, though, only required two things. The first were the contact details for the victim's parents, and a copy of the birth certificate. For bureaucratic reasons, more than anything else, the team needed a copy of Noor's birth certificate to clarify his identity.

As promised, she faxed a copy of Noor's birth certificate, which confirmed that Noor had lied all along.

The document revealed that he had been born on 7 July 1965 in the Lamh District in the Coast

Province in Kenya, and named Sheilila Salim. Among the general information it provided was the name and address of his mother, Somoe Bakari Shigoo. It stated that she lived in Mombassa.

This information opened up yet another line of investigation for McDonnell. He now began searching for the mother, whom he presumed was desperately worried about her son. It took him a further week to locate her, but when he did, he was told she spoke no English. He began searching for an interpreter to conduct the dialogue.

*****

At the beginning of his interview with Linda, Mangan could never have envisaged what would have happened. Linda, trapped in a nightmare of depression and guilt, had confessed. The investigation team had established, with as much certainty as possible, what had happened on the night of the killing; in other words, how the victim died, at whose hands and why.

The significance of this was not easily calculated. Mangan knew her decision to confess had been the beginning of a long process that would eventually result in her being charged.

No one outside the team had known about Linda's decision to confess; or the contents of the statements she made. These had been transcribed and assembled into a book of evidence by Dan Kenna, a detective on the team. His forensic approach to the accuracy of the case reports ensured the body of evidence that was assembled was watertight. The relevant paperwork on the inquiry had been passed to the Director of Public Prosecutions by Mangan, in accordance with procedure.

The evidence against Linda was as clear as it was comprehensive. She had made confession after confession admitting her role in the killing. The confessions, dictated in her own words, were supported by hard evidence that had been found at the relevant scenes.

Mangan himself had attached a written report stating there was no doubt about Linda's guilt. He recommended that she be charged.

And so, six months after Noor's body parts were first discovered, a direction to prefer a murder charge was issued by Robert Sheehan, from the offices of the Director of Public Prosecutions to Detective Superintendent John McKeown, the police officer with overall responsibility for the investigation. Mangan received the instruction on 13 September.

He decided to make the arrest himself. He knew Linda, and in a way, she would have expected it. It was Mangan and Hickey whom she had made the confessions to. The low key meetings with the killer had achieved what the team had set out to accomplish; that was to solve the case, though anyone familiar with the events of the past weeks also knew that no member of the team, least of all Mangan, relished the task. Linda, as Charlotte, was a product of a society that had shaped their personalities.

The actual arrest took place the following day, hours after Mangan swore an oath seeking an arrest warrant before Judge Hugh O'Donnell in the Dublin District Court. The judge issued the warrant in private so as not to alert anyone to the unfolding drama.

When Mangan took possession of the arrest warrant, his first priority was to ensure that Linda's children did not pay witness to their mother's arrest. This was imperative. There was a genuine wish that everything should run as smoothly as possible, but no one wished to affect the children. The detectives on the team understood the importance of this.

The team arrived at the family home in Kilclare Gardens the following morning, shortly after 10am, when Linda's children had left for school.

When Mangan arrived at the door of the council house, Linda instinctively knew the reason for the visit. When she opened the door; she didn't say a word at first, but listened impassively as Mangan placed his hand on her arm, and administered a caution. She was stunned, but in some ways nonplussed; then she began to cry. In a few short moments her world began to fall apart.

Mangan treaded as softly as he could but he had a job to do; he asked her to get some things together and offered to help her get ready.

Her response took him by surprise. Struggling to pull herself together, she said she had packed in anticipation of this day, since the first day they had met. At that moment, she looked distraught.

There was nothing that any member of the team could say or do to console her, which is why they moved as quickly as possible to take her into custody.

Moments later, Mangan asked if she understood what had been said. He was referring to the caution. She nodded, prompting one of the team to hand her a tissue. He then directed her towards the door and into a waiting patrol car.

Before they left the house, Mangan rang Kevin Tunney, a solicitor from Tallaght who specialised in criminal law. He explained the purpose of the call, and passed his phone to Linda, who was now his prisoner. She had a brief conversation with the solicitor.

When she had gathered what few possessions she had, Linda was placed in a patrol car that took her to Mountjoy Garda Station. At that moment, she felt the end of the world had come.

*****

The group arrived in Mountjoy Station at 10.55am. On arrival, she was processed by the Duty Sergeant who took her name, details and age. When this process was completed at 11.22am, Sergeant Shay Roche formally charged her with Noor's murder as set out on charge sheet No. 417567. The details of the charges were as follows:

'That you the said accused on or about 20 March 2005 at Flat 1, 17 Richmond Cottages, Ballybough, Dublin 1, in said District Court area of Dublin Metropolitan District did murder one Sheilila Salim, otherwise known as Farah Swaleh Noor, contrary to common law.'

Her only response was to say 'No'. This was of course in accordance with her legal instructions.

The next stage of the process was a formal court appearance at Court No. 44 in the Dublin District

Court. It was here that she appeared before Judge Miriam Malone. Linda was not asked to address the court, apart from confirming her name.

Instead Mangan gave evidence of the arrest, which was perfunctory. Judge Malone then requested that she be medically examined and treated as appropriate. The hearing was over in minutes. She was next remanded in custody to appear the following Wednesday.

*****

Linda was not to know her mother had been arrested in Carlow and was still in custody. She had been re-arrested under Section 10 of the Criminal Justice Act 1987, and detained once again for the murder of Farah Swaleh Noor. This time, the investigation team had new information.

Kathleen remained calm while in custody. She was polite to her interviewers, and never obnoxious.

During that period, she was subjected to a series of interviews aimed at enticing her to make a full statement about her knowledge of Noor's untimely death.

Detective Sergeant Gerard McDonnell and Detective Garda Patrick Keegan were tasked with conducting most of this interview. While she spoke freely about how Noor subjected her to extreme violence, she did not confess to anything; though she did reveal more information about her relationship with Noor.

In the course of the interview, she claimed that Noor had threatened to kill her the week before he died.

According to a statement she made, she said: 'I was getting my Social money for Farah and myself. I said to Farah, "I can't keep collecting for you as you are working and if the Social find out my money will be stopped." So I went to the Social Welfare and I told them I was not with Farah anymore, and I told them to stop his money. I asked them for a letter and they gave me a letter,' she said.

'Farah rang me that night and he told me I was a fucking liar, that I had his money. I told him I had a letter to say I wasn't getting his money. I gave him the letter. He looked at it, read it, and said all I was was a fucking cunt, and said I wouldn't get away with this.'

She maintained this altercation took place a week before he died.

'He said to me, I am going to fucking kill you, just like I did with that whore in Dun Laoghaire,' she added.

The fact that Noor had claimed responsibility for Raonaid Murray's murder, prompted the detectives to ask what he meant.

'I don't know what he meant,' replied Kathleen.

'Was he talking about Raonaid Murray?'

'Yes, her,' she said.

'I asked Farah not to kill me as I didn't do anything on him. He started beating me and he threw me in the bedroom, in No. 17 Richmond Cottages. Then he tried to smother me with pillows and I couldn't breathe. Then he jumped on top of me.

'I don't know where I got the strength from but I kicked him in the stomach, and he came off me. Then, when he got up, I made a 999 call and I said I would ring the police.

'He ran out to the kitchen, and got a knife. He said I am going to chop you up into little pieces and eat you. I said, "You can't. If Charlotte rings and I don't answer she will know there is a problem and come to the house." He said, "Kathy, I am going to chop you up into little pieces, put you in the fridge and eat you piece by piece." He said no one will ever find you because I will tell them you fucked off.'

She continued: 'So then he sits down, and started thinking, and calmed down. He said that if I ever told the police he would kill me or my family.

'I told him to leave my flat and there would be no problem. So he took some stuff and he went.'

She maintained Noor moved out the week before 20 March. She elaborated further, claiming that she asked him to return the keys.

'I said, "Farah can I have the keys of the house please?" He said "No," he was keeping the keys. I told him to keep the keys and to fuck off. He then said "You will never get away from me."'

There is no doubt that she was living in fear of her life, though she still didn't make any admissions. Instead she maintained she had done nothing wrong, and that Noor had left her. After her period of detention ended, she was released without charge.

*****

That wasn't the end of the matter. The investigation continued apace; in fact Linda's appearance in court gave it fresh impetus. The inquiry had been written off as one that would never come to a successful conclusion. The direction to charge Linda with murder had dispelled that myth.

In this whirlwind of activity, McDonnell had continued in his efforts to try to locate the victim's mother. He accomplished this task on 23 September, when Somoe Bakari Said received a call from a translator he hired. Through the translator McDonnell learned much about Noor's history; for a start, he was told Noor had called himself Farah all his life. The mother explained the name was one that his father's family had called him since he was a boy. But there was more. His mother said she had known that something was wrong when her son had stopped calling.

She initially thought he was ill, or possibly in prison, because he called every Saturday without fail, and had kept her informed of his new life, including his relationship with Kathleen.

The phone call was a traumatic one. The image of her son, stabbed in the neck, and dying slowly in Ireland, far away from her home, had haunted her. She had many sleepless nights. The only thing that gave her some consolation was her grandchildren, and the memory of the son she loved.

McDonnell was struck by her sadness, and asked if she had ever spoken to Kathleen. The answer took him by surprise. The family had.

In an ironic twist, she often sent Noor clothes to sustain him in Ireland. In fact, she had sent one on 3 March; furthermore her son had called on 7 March to see if she had sent it, as he had still not received it.

As she couldn't speak English, Noor's cousin, Lulu Swaleh, had called Kathleen on 10 March to ask if the parcel had arrived. Kathleen had replied that it had, but claimed that Noor had left her for another woman.

The family did not know what to make of her statement but accepted it on face value. They had not heard from him since.

Perhaps the most saddening part of the call was her recollection of the last time she spoke to her son. McDonnell listened in silence as she recounted that conversation, which took place sometime between 15 and 20 March.

The memory of that conversation was clear in her mind. Her son, she said without contradiction, had been distant, almost as if he was trying to say sorry for things that had happened in the past. She sensed trouble; something sinister. She woke feeling troubled by the conversation for no clear reason. Soon she would learn the terrible fate that had befallen her son.

She went on to tell the interpreter that Lulu Swaleh, her nephew, had called Kathleen in the months that followed the disappearance asking about Noor, but she had maintained that he had left her.

McDonnell took down the details as best he could as the interpreter relayed the times, dates and her recollections of the long distance calls.

There was one that was of particular interest to the detective sergeant. One night around 2am, Kathleen rang Lulu in a distressed state, speaking about Farah. She had been incoherent and didn't make sense. Although he wasn't sure why, Noor's cousin felt that something was seriously wrong.

The call remained etched in his mind because the family had never heard from Kathleen again, nor Noor, whom had vanished without trace from their lives.

CHAPTER EIGHT

'Falsehood is easy, truth so difficult.'

- George Eliot

THE APPEARANCE OF Linda in the District Court, on murder charges, terrified Charlotte. She felt weak and vulnerable but she also felt this growing sense of unease. Like Linda, she couldn't sleep at night and found it difficult to maintain any semblance of normality in the face of extreme internal pressure and depression. She too had flashbacks of the night she killed Noor and dismembered his body. She played it over again and again in her mind.

She couldn't help but think of her own terrifying predicament; the weakness of her position was now apparent. If Linda had been charged with murder, she knew it was only a matter of time before she was re-arrested and brought to court. No matter what way she examined the situation, no matter what the context, she came to the conclusion that she was doomed.

There is no doubt that her father attempted to convince her to confess, but she was too afraid. She was terrified.

Whether it was because she had physically killed Noor, and been the instigator of the dismemberment that she chose to remain silent will never be known. Matters were not helped because she was now leading a dysfunctional life, moving between homes and taking drugs. This left her in a humiliating position insofar as her immediate family did not know of her problems, and she desperately wanted to get on with her life. She was a girl in need of urgent help.

She hoped against hope that she would be spared further inquiries from the Garda. This belief, which was no more than an idle hope, was encouraged when she learned from Linda that she had been charged on the basis of the statements she had made incriminating herself.

To survive mentally, Charlotte convinced herself that she was untouchable; though in reality she was just as vulnerable as her sister.

Although she had been arrested in August, she had been freed without charge. She interpreted this as a good omen—a sign there was no evidence against her. What she didn't understand was that Linda's statements constituted new evidence which permitted the team to arrest her for the same offence, once more.

The inevitable happened on the morning of 17 October, almost four weeks after Linda's court appearance. Charlotte had gotten into more trouble. While she had vanished for a time, the team had managed to locate her.

She visibly weakened when she saw them. This time, Hickey was the arresting officer. There was a warrant out for her arrest in relation to a number of minor charges. Like Linda weeks earlier, she too was taken to Mountjoy Station for interrogation.

She was at times polite and friendly, but at the same time she could be aggressive. In some ways, she would show disdain for the detectives. They interpreted this as bravado; an act she engaged in to make herself look hard when she was frightened.

This time, the interview was conducted by Detective Garda Mike Smyth and McDonnell. It began at 4.21pm that afternoon. Charlotte at first seemed to co-operate but it soon became clear that she was lying about much of what she said.

The interrogation began with McDonnell and Smyth explaining the reason why she had been arrested. This was explained to her in a slow and methodical way. They said they believed that she was in a position to help the investigation into Noor's death.

Charlotte answered that she was, which came as a surprise. Given that Linda had made a full confession, the interrogators asked if she wanted them to contact someone.

'No Linda knows I'm here,' she answered. She then said she didn't want a solicitor. The interrogation then proceeded.

McDonnell led the questions.

'You were arrested earlier in relation to this?'

'Yes.'

'Were you aware we had a warrant for your re-arrest?'

'No, I wasn't aware of that,' she said, which she wasn't.

'When you were in the first time you answered our questions, what do you say about that?'

'I did know about it, I was lying,' she said.

'Are you prepared to tell us the whole truth?'

This was a typical garda ploy to put the suspect on a firm footing to be discredited if she lied. However, it also gave Charlotte the opportunity to tell her version of what happened, or to contest her recollection of the night's events against Linda's, if she so wished.

While McDonnell and Smyth may have initially thought she was about to confess; they knew this was not to be when she answered their next question.

Without fear of contradiction, Charlotte said she was now going to tell the truth. Then, she took a deep breath and lied.

'I am but I wasn't in the flat when it happened.'

The two detectives never flinched, nor showed their disbelief at her denial. Instead they proceeded methodically.

'You were out?'

'Yeah me and Linda, from 10 till 5 or 6 the next morning.'

'Where?'

'Around town, drinking.'

'You are aware Linda has told us she was in the flat?'

'I am, I don't know why she told you that.'

'When did you last see Farah Noor?'

'Just before we left the flat on 20 March.'

'Do you know what night that was?'

'No.'

'How do you know it was the 20 March though?'

'Cause it's my birthday the next day,' she retorted.

The interview continued in this vein. Her denials sounded more pitiful than contrived because Charlotte knew her sister had confessed, and furthermore that Linda's statement had been corroborated by evidence found at the crime scenes.

Still she maintained she had left the flat with Linda at about 10pm, and they had spent the night drinking on the boardwalk.

It became clear that she was not just trying to protect herself; she was trying to protect Linda. Given that Charlotte had initially attacked Noor for his indiscretion in physically touching Linda, this made every sense.

Her story, though, only made sense in her own mind, as she hadn't thought it through. It was full of inconsistencies and contradictions, which were clear.

McDonnell, who had dealt with scores of hardened killers in his career, never stopped Charlotte from contradicting herself, even at times when he knew she was lying outright. Smyth also remained impassive.

She continued to lie, claiming that when she and Linda had returned to their mother's flat the following morning; they found Noor dead, and his body dismembered.

Contrary to this, in the statement she made later, which was produced in court, she claimed that when she came home, she found her mother covered in blood.

She said at first that she thought her mother had been assaulted by the dead man, but then her mother said she had killed him with a hammer and by cutting his throat, before chopping up his body.

Asked about her sister's earlier statements, her answer was categorical. 'I just think Linda is mad for saying things she didn't do.'

There was purpose in this statement. It was designed to make the detectives second guess themselves and wonder if Linda had indeed told the truth.

The next question was the only logical one the interrogators could ask. If this was the case, why had Linda lied?

'Because we promised my ma we would say we did it,' Charlotte answered.

She didn't stop there. She next admitted that she had helped dump the body parts, and took money from Noor's bank account, but maintained that she had killed no one, and neither had Linda. This left the detectives in a situation where they could only shrug their shoulders. However, her denials presented them with an opportunity to take the interrogation in another direction. If this was Charlotte's story; then they would test its veracity. They began by asking simple questions; they asked her where they had gone after they left Richmond Cottages.

'Name one place that I can find you on video that night between 10pm and 6am?' they asked.

'The boardwalk,' she said.

'So if I look at the video I'll find you?'

'Yeah.'

'That's simply not true?'

'It is.'

'Why does Linda's story gel and yours is full of inconsistencies?'

'I don't ... ' Charlotte looked towards the ground. She couldn't make eye contact. Inside, she was panicking.

'Did your mother ever tell you of assaults?'

'Yes. He broke her ribs,' she said, trying to rescue the situation.

'Were they arguing earlier in the day?'

'Yes.'

'So you are telling us you left whilst your mother and Farah were arguing?'

'I was sick listening to them.'

'Did your mother tell you that Farah had threatened to kill her two weeks previously?'

She looked up momentarily.

'No.'

'Did you know that your mother was being beaten?'

'Yes but not since they came to Dublin,' she said, again refusing to make eye contact.

They next pursued a line of questioning that was to the forefront of their minds. The team had received the specific details of the telephone traffic between the phones of the main suspects at crucial times. These showed that John Mulhall Snr and his wife had talked on the night of Noor's death.

'Did your father have much contact with your mother?'

Charlotte was surprised by the question, but answered:

'No.'

'Would they ring each other?'

'Not unless he was looking for me.'

'Are you close to your father?'

'Yes.'

'Did you tell him about this?'

She lied. 'No,' was her final answer.

'Tell anyone?'

'No.'

'Do you feel sorry about all this?'

'Yeah.'

'If you were going to defend your mother over this why didn't you go to the police?'

'I just didn't.'

'Were you staying in Richmond Cottages?'

'I was.'

'What happened to Farah's ATM card and mobile?' they asked.

'Mammy gave me his ATM card and I took money out.'

'You say the bags with Farah's body were in the flat when you got back?'

'Yeah, in the bathroom.'

'Did you bring them down to the canal?'

'Yeah about 7.30am.'

'Where was the head?'

'I don't know, me ma had it.'

'And his penis?'

'Don't know.'

'What kind of bags was the body in?'

'Sports bags, three.'

'What happened to them?'

'We dumped the parts and brought them back to the flat, ma put them in black bags I think.'

The next question threw her but also revealed her own complicity in the killing and dismemberment.

'What did she say she cut him up with?'

'A knife.'

'How did she overpower him?'

'She hit him with a hammer.'

Without warning, they then returned to her alibi.

'What did you drink while you were out of the house?'

'Vodka and cans.'

'So you went around the town for eight hours, drinking and taking heroin?'

'Yeah,' she answered.

The detectives were skilled at their job. They changed the line of questioning again; this broke her concentration momentarily.

'Where was Farah's head?'

'Out the back in a sports bag. A small one.'

'Where did it end up?'

'I don't know. She said she would get rid of it.'

This question had thrown her. Linda had taken the head. She knew this. More importantly, she knew the detectives in the room knew this.

'Can you tell us any person, anything, any phone call you made, while you were out that night?'

'No.'

'And Linda does not say she was out?'

Charlotte made a pitiful sight and her repeated denials were pathetic; not because they were easily dismissed; but because they were sad and misguided. Charlotte was lying in a misguided attempt to protect her sister, who had already accepted her fate and the consequences of her actions.

Inside though, she knew she was fighting a losing battle.

Finally, when she had done everything that she could, she broke. The catalyst was a simple question that McDonnell posed; he once more asked her why Linda's story gelled when hers was full of inconsistencies.

She had no answer because there was none.

In an attempt to show her some kindness, the detectives asked her once again if she wanted to speak to a solicitor. She declined the offer.

However, the question had some impact on her. Her answers became short and she now stared at the ground, deep in thought. When they mentioned Linda again, tears welled up in her eyes.

McDonnell spoke calmly and directly to her, this time looking her straight in the eye, almost encouraging her to confess, for her own benefit, if not Linda's.

Rather than allowing her to tell more lies, he confronted her with the undeniable truth, making a specific reference to Linda's statement, which said she had disposed of the head.

Charlotte tutted in response, in much the same way as a teenager does when scolded by a parent.

'Why have you not spoken to a solicitor?'

'Don't know.'

'But it's a very serious charge?'

'Don't know.'

'But you know it's your right?'

'Yeah.'

'Did you look for a solicitor before?'

'No.'

'Do you still feel you don't require a solicitor?'

'Yeah.'

'Do you want us to contact one for you?'

'No.'

'Do you want to tell us the truth?'

Charlotte hesitated for a moment; she stared at the floor once more, then took a deep breath and began to sob. Tears streamed down her face. Then she said the following:

'Everything that Linda says happened.'

The weakness of her position was apparent; not alone could she not tell another lie; she didn't want to. Like Linda, she had had enough. Noor had haunted her.

'What do you want to say about what you said earlier?'

Fighting back the tears, the only word she could muster was, 'Sorry.'

'Were you doing it to protect Linda?'

She was incapable of speech now. She nodded in reply, through her tears, struggling to speak or focus her mind on the questions she was being asked. She cut a poignant figure in the interrogation suite. She did not fit the profile of a ruthless killer; she was the opposite. She was a damaged woman.

The team began to ask her a series of simple questions, which she answered honestly and as best she could. She continued to cry, in much the same way that Linda had confessed.

'Go through it in your own time,' the gardaí prompted her.

'We were all drinking, Farah didn't want to take E, Ma put it in his drink. He grabbed Linda by the arm, everyone was just arguing … Linda hit him with the hammer, this was in the bedroom. I can't remember everything; I stabbed him in the neck. I don't remember how he died in the bedroom but he was dead,' she said.

'Did you ring anyone?'

'I don't remember, we didn't know what to do; cut him up, we did.'

'Where?'

'In the bathroom.'

'What time?'

'I don't know.'

'How did you cut him up?'

'With the knife and the hammer. I would cut him with the kitchen knife, Linda used the hammer.'

'Did you strip him naked?'

'Yes.'

'Do you remember his penis being cut off?'

'Yes.'

'And his head?'

'Yes.'

'What happened his head?'

'The three of us left it in a park beside the Square, but Linda moved it.'

'Are you prepared to give this in a statement form?'

She said yes. Like Linda, she refused to take a break from the interrogation and insisted on completing her statement. She signed it at 6.15pm that same evening after agreeing it was correct. When she had finished, she cried some more, and was led away to a cell.

She was uncertain about what she had done but she was inwardly relieved.

Mangan had been made aware of the confession and immediately contacted the DPP's office seeking an instruction. This was duly given. In essence, Charlotte's statement corroborated her sister Linda's version of events, which had already passed the legal requirements needed for a murder charge.

She was in the same agitated state later that night when she was formally charged with murder. Although she had expected it, it still came as a shock to her. She was a young girl who should have been enjoying her life. Those on the investigation team couldn't help but wonder about the journey she had travelled, which had led her to this sad point. She was taken to the Dublin District Court the following morning where she was formally charged with Noor's murder. She appeared before Judge Conal Gibbons, who remanded her in custody.

*****

At first it was impossible to tell whether John Mulhall Snr had been involved in the killing or not. The series of calls he made and received on the night of the killing proved that he had communicated with his daughters.

In other words, the question remained: could he have helped dispose of evidence or the body itself? Linda and Charlotte had both denied his involvement, and even his knowledge of the horrific fate that had befallen Noor. However, this made no sense. But the detective team had to act on what they knew to be true.

Mangan, privately, was of the opinion that Mulhall Snr had known what happened, though possibly hadn't gotten involved. His actions were those of a father terrified for his two daughters' welfare.

The question remained unanswered and was conspicuous by its absence from the book of evidence that Kenna had carefully scrutinised in the incident room.

It was for this reason that Mangan and Hickey arrested him a second time on the morning of 10 November by arrangement, and took him to Kilmainham Garda Station. It was here that they asked him to be honest and reveal why he had spoken to his daughters on the night of the killing. To Mangan and Hickey, his actions made no sense; they knew he no longer cared for Kathleen.

For the benefit of the video recorder in the interrogation suite, Mulhall spent an hour denying he had travelled from his home to Richmond Cottages. However, moments after he had managed to convince the detectives that he had not been inside the flat, he confessed that he had. Mangan had to pinch himself when he made the admission.

Mulhall Snr, trying to be as honest as he could, said he had been called and told that Noor was dead. He hadn't believed it, but then had a terrible sense of foreboding, which caused him to drive to the city.

He recounted how he had arrived at the flat expecting to find Noor badly beaten, perhaps injured, or at worst unconscious.

The detectives listened in astonishment as he explained what happened next. It was noteworthy that he was the only one present who was not under the influence of drugs.

He recalled how he had looked for Farah in the bedroom, and noticed nothing untoward. Then he spoke about the bin liner that contained the body parts. Mangan knew by his body language that he was telling the truth. The memory of the night was etched in his mind.

Satisfied he had told the truth, and lied in order to protect himself and his daughters, he was freed. Mangan, in turn, told him to take care. No one realised how distraught Mulhall Snr had grown since the killing; he was genuinely horrified over what had happened to Noor. The unspeakable act of dismemberment had shocked him to his core. No matter what way he looked at the situation, he could not comprehend what Linda and Charlotte had done.

It was no secret that he had encouraged them to confess. More than anything, he had wanted them to do the right thing. He was convinced that if they told the truth, the gardaí, perhaps even a jury, would understand the traumatic events that had unfolded. Mulhall Snr gave the impression that he was tormented by guilt and a growing depression.

The more he thought about their predicament, the more he realised they were themselves trapped in a living nightmare. The strain of living with this knowledge took its toll. Soon he found it too much to bear, and with the turmoil of this, three months after his 53rd birthday he tragically reached his limit and took his own life. He hanged himself in Phoenix Park.

His untimely death was perhaps the greatest tragedy that could have befallen Linda and Charlotte. He had been the breadwinner for the family, but also its rock; a man who held it together. He had, in many peoples' opinion, reformed his life and conquered his own demons, only to be confronted by others.

He was buried in a ceremony which members of the detective unit attended.

Linda didn't blame herself; she was not responsible. Heartbroken and at the end of her tether, she called Mangan in desperation; she was falling apart. That her father had committed suicide, although horrific, wasn't at the forefront of her mind. In truth, she was now thinking about her own future and her family. That Christmas was an ordeal for the Mulhall family. In many ways it symbolised the unfolding tragedy of nightmarish proportions that was engulfing them. Linda would later try to articulate the utter despair that overcame her. She managed to hold her life together for her children but the façade was nothing more than a guise. Charlotte was also distraught. No amount of drugs and alcohol could make the pain and hurt go away. It was infectious.

*****

The funeral of John Mulhall was followed three months later by that of Noor's. After every effort had been made to find his skull, the body was released for burial.

Teams of search dogs and gardaí had combed the hinterland around Killinarden Hill without any success. Eventually the search was wound down and the funeral arrangements made.

About 40 people gathered at Glasnevin Cemetery to take part in a Muslim ceremony to mark the violent life of Farah Swaleh Noor, or

Sheilila Salim. No members of his family were in attendance; they were too poor to afford the flight, or pay the cost of repatriating his body to Kenya. In any event, it is preferred for a Muslim to be buried where he or she has died, and not be transported to another location or country.

Instead his remains were shrouded in preparation for burial as is custom, in a manner similar to how Muslims make ablutions for prayer. His body was then wrapped in sheets of white cloth, or the *kafan*.

He was then transported to the site of the funeral prayer, *salat-l-janazah*, which in the circumstances was Staffords Funeral Home. An Imam stood in front of the deceased, facing away from the worshippers, and said a few short words; the remainder of the funeral prayers were recited by the mourners in total silence.

He was next taken to the cemetery for burial. His former partner and mother of his son attended his burial, and said prayers for his soul. He was laid in the grave on his right side, facing Mecca.

It made a poignant scene. After he was laid to rest, his friends and other mourners filled in the grave by hand.

Mangan, Hickey and the others on the team stood in attendance to pay their respects. When the burial process had been completed, his friends

Right: About 40 people gathered at Glasnevin Cemetery in Dublin for the funeral of Noor. No members of his family were able to attend, as they were too poor to afford the flight to Ireland.

Below: Linda's legal team argued that she was paramount in solving the crime, given her confession to detectives.

Charlotte had a six month old baby at this time, and would later request that her baby be brought into the prison with her.

This page © Courtpix

Top: Mr Justice Paul Carney, who presided over the trial. He described it as 'the most grotesque case of killing that has occurred within my professional lifetime.'
Above left: George Birmingham SC for the prosecution.
Above right: Brendan Grehan SC, defence for Linda Mulhall, who argued a defence of provocation on his client's behalf.

the trial went on, the
otion and tension
to Charlotte and
ecially Linda.
She had admitted to
ectives that she was
nted by the face of
or after his death.

This page © Collins Agency / Garrett White

On 4 December 2006 Charlotte Mulhall was sentenced to life for the
murder of Farah Swaleh Noor. After 18 hours of deliberation over
three days, Linda Mulhall's defence of provocation was accepted
and she was sentenced to 15 years for manslaughter. She wept as her
sentence was read out in court.

took branches from nearby yew trees and placed them around the grave, along with large stones. To them, the stones and branches signified Allah and his mercy for the deceased.

Noor had come to Ireland with hopes of building a new life, but had not succeeded. Instead he had become a violent alcoholic who preyed on vulnerable women. This remained his legacy.

CHAPTER NINE

'Fear follows crime, and is its punishment.'

- Voltaire

INSTEAD OF FEELING hopeful about the chances of an acquittal, Linda Mulhall was terrified; more than anything she was fearful of losing her children. She was not one of those women who could put such fears to the back of her mind; instead she dwelled on them. The thought of losing her children consumed her in a way that only a mother can be affected by the loss of a child; she felt that no one understood.

Charlotte had been remanded in custody to Mountjoy Prison because she broke the conditions of her bail. She had stopped signing on at the nominated Garda Station. Linda had been given her freedom. It was during this time, in the weeks before the trial, that she descended into a deeper depression.

It should be noted that her mother, Kathleen, had since left Ireland. She had moved to Britain, where she had begun a new life in Birmingham; then she had vanished without trace.

Linda hadn't broken the conditions of her bail, but there were times when she wanted to. Instead, she drank and took more drugs to escape from the life that offered her no peace and to ease the pain that swelled inside her heart.

Throughout her life, the only thing she had treasured were her children, whom she loved beyond question. Though she knew she would have to be separated from them at some point, she could not accept it. She simply wasn't ready to go to prison.

Drugs and alcohol had always been her way of dealing with problems. She had always switched off when confronted by bad news. However, it now impacted on her forthcoming trial.

*****

By this time, the sisters had been given legal aid, and had eminent teams of barristers and solicitors appointed to represent them. Linda had retained Kevin Tunney, the solicitor whom Mangan had called on the morning of her arrest. He had subsequently appointed a legal executive from his firm to help prepare her defence. This was a high profile trial and Tunney was leaving nothing to chance.

His firm did everything to encourage Linda to help herself, but given the circumstances, this proved a difficult exercise.

In the weeks preceding the trial that had been due to start on 1 October in the Central Criminal Court before Justice Paul Carney, the legal team had slowly come to realise that Linda was seriously affected by drug taking. In fact, she was in the depths of utter despair.

The solicitor immediately contacted the two barristers they had hired to represent their client. These were Brendan Grehan, a senior counsel, and Kieran Kelly, a barrister, and informed them of the situation. Left with no other choice, they set about preparing the best defence they could in the circumstances.

Then disaster struck on the opening morning of the trial in Court No. 2, which lies off the round hall in the Four Courts complex.

On that morning, it was packed to capacity with journalists, gardaí, and curious onlookers.

Silence descended as Judge Carney entered the courtroom at 11am precisely.

Although there are numerous judges in the High Court, Justice Paul Carney was without doubt the most high profile. A man with an undeniable work ethic, he had presided over most of the controversial trials to come before the courts. He was known as a straight talker who didn't mince his words.

It was at this point that Judge Carney's notice was drawn to Linda's absence. She had vanished though Charlotte was present.

In the previous hours, Linda's legal team and Mangan had attempted to call her. This had proven a fruitless exercise.

Moments later, Judge Carney was formally notified of her absence, forcing him to issue a bench warrant for her arrest. Mangan and the detective team were, once again, tasked with locating her.

The judge then adjourned the trial. It was the wish of all sides to have the two individual cases tried together. On leaving the court, Mangan went straight to a house in Tallaght where they knew

Linda had been staying, but she wasn't there. Every time someone dialled her phone, it continued to ring out. Nor did she respond to texts.

Left with no other choice, the team circulated a secret Garda bulletin giving her details and picture to gardaí on duty at the ports and airports. She was to be arrested on sight, the bulletin warned.

Later that day, Mangan received the news that an officer on duty in Dun Laoghaire had reported seeing a woman, fitting her description, take that morning's departure to Wales.

This was a disastrous course of action for Linda to take. Mangan moved swiftly to arrange to have her intercepted, if indeed it was her.

Trying to work out the best possible thing to do, he tried to contact her once more. This time, he sent her a text, and requested a notification report that would categorically show whether she received the text or not.

Moments after he pressed send, his phone screen flickered, signalling the text had been delivered, which could only mean one thing: that she was still in Dublin.

After 24 hours of texts and calls, and after much persuasion by Mangan, Linda was convinced to give herself up. Eventually, she agreed.

Later that night, the team met her outside a house in Tallaght. She arrived looking destitute, with two of her children. She was in floods of tears. In fact, she was inconsolable and on the verge of a breakdown.

The youngsters were also distraught. One of them approached Mangan and asked him to look after his mother, before shaking the detective's hand. Linda then held her boy, and with every ounce of strength she had in her body, told him that she loved him. There was nothing that any of those present could do or say to change the course of what had to happen.

Trying to compose herself, Linda took her belongings—which included some clothes and soft toys from her childhood—from the taxi she had arrived in, and handed these to the detectives. She hugged her children once more, kissed them and told them she loved them, and then let them go. The scene was one of utter tragedy and despair.

Those who know her say she no longer cared for herself at this stage. In the deepest grief, she sat into a patrol car and was taken to the Women's Prison in Mountjoy in preparation for the next day.

When she appeared in court the following morning, Grehan made an application to have the trial date moved. Judge Carney listened attentively to the submission.

He watched for reaction from the prosecution, which was led by George Birmingham, a senior counsel, and Úna Ní Raifeartaigh, a second barrister on the team.

It should be noted that Charlotte's legal team were also present. Her solicitor was John O'Doherty, a renowned practitioner of criminal law. Her senior counsel was Isobel Kennedy, who was working alongside Sean Gillane, a barrister.

Grehan set out the reasons for the application. Tunney had arranged for her to be examined by a forensic psychiatrist who practiced in Dublin; Dr Brian McCaffery.

The psychiatrist concluded, without any hesitation, that she was not fit to stand trial. She was on drugs and drinking large amounts of alcohol. He had informed Tunney of his opinion and was now in court to give evidence.

After some discussions, and considering the psychiatric evaluation furnished by Dr McCaffery, the team wanted to have her trial delayed, ideally for a month.

However, the judge ruled against him. A month was out of the question, but he did offer Linda a week.

It was noteworthy that he offered to allow both Linda and Charlotte take short breaks from the trial, if they required them; he then adjourned the trial once more.

When it resumed on 9 October—almost a year and a half after Noor had been brutally killed—a jury was empanelled. Though it would be another two days before the trial began hearing evidence.

*****

When the trial did eventually open, Linda stood alongside Charlotte. The two sisters denied the charge of murder and pleaded not guilty, despite their confessions. Linda looked worn out and tired.

The trial opened with the usual formality. Birmingham first outlined the facts of the case against the Mulhall sisters. Still trapped in the throes of a depression, Linda listened to the story that she was all too familiar with.

Birmingham spoke without any pomposity. He said it was the prosecution's case that at a flat in Richmond Cottages, Noor was murdered by the two women.

'Charlotte Mulhall had a knife and Linda Mulhall wielded a hammer with which she struck him a significant number of times, on or about the head.'

He continued: 'Members of the Garda Sub-Aqua Unit retrieved parts of the body in the canal but what they retrieved did not constitute the body in its entirety, because missing was the head, and also missing was the deceased's penis.'

The jury—comprising six men and six women —looked on as he explained how Noor had been in a relationship with their mother Kathleen, which the barrister described as 'fraught' and 'stormy'.

After he outlined how Noor's body had been discovered, Birmingham described how an examination of the body revealed 22 stab wounds and injuries to 'pretty well all' of the internal organs.

Birmingham didn't overstate the facts of the case, or linger on any specific details; in many ways he didn't need to. The details of the killing, which were written word for word by the assembled media, horrified those listening. There was absolute silence in the courtroom, such was the atmosphere.

He continued to address the jury, stating it was the prosecution's argument that the body had been dismembered to make the identification more difficult. Birmingham, though, explained that his case largely rested on the confessions the Mulhall sisters had made. Both sisters, he said, had admitted their involvement in the killing and the disposal of the body.

In the dock, Linda and Charlotte looked on, bewildered and partly confused. Though Linda had the outward appearance of a terrified woman, Charlotte looked more relaxed; but this was an act. She too was terrified. She was a new mother. She had given birth to a baby boy six months earlier. She too longed to be with her child; the thought of separation was so much that she blocked it out, according to those who know her. Her outward appearance led many present to think she didn't care; but this couldn't have been further from the truth.

In closing his speech, Birmingham said: 'It remains to this day that the head of Mr Noor has not been located.'

Everyone knew this was the case but the comment made an impact on everyone present; it was shocking because it was the truth.

*****

The trial progressed in a usual fashion the next morning. Birmingham began by calling witnesses to give less than contestable evidence. This evidence was standard, and concerned the details surrounding the discovery of the body.

Mohammed Ali Abu Bakaar, the man who had met Noor on the day he died, was among these witnesses. He explained to Birmingham that he had known the victim from the east-African coastline, where the two had worked on fishing boats. He recounted his last conversation with his old friend, and described how Noor was prone to heavy drinking.

He recalled, as best he could, how he told Noor to go home because he was drunk.

'I call him to talk to him because I know after a few drinks, Farah, anything can happen to him. I always do that to people I know when I see them in that condition,' he said.

While the two defendants had two separate legal teams, the barristers sometimes liaised. Grehan had paid careful attention to the evidence. When he rose to his feet, he asked Bakaar about Noor's alcoholism.

It was no secret that both teams wanted to portray Noor as the violent thug he was. This could only help their case. Linda's team particularly saw the benefit of this. They argued that Linda was not a murderer; but had reasonable grounds for provocation, which they hoped would lead to an acquittal, or a manslaughter charge. With this in mind, Grehan asked if he knew whether Noor's personality changed dramatically when he drank alcohol.

'I never lasted the whole night with him,' was Bakaar's answer.

*****

The first week of the trial had been calamitous for Linda and Charlotte. Though, as the days passed, they appeared to have accepted their fate and how best to handle the situation. Charlotte more than Linda settled into the routine, though sometimes her eyes wandered. She rarely looked at any of the witnesses, but sneaked glances at them when the opportunity presented itself. Linda, though, sometimes looked distant. She constantly thought of her children, and how they were faring, though she spoke to them everyday without fail. More than anything, this kept her going. She was also consoled by the fact that she knew that whatever verdict was reached, it would bring closure to this dark episode in her life. In some ways, amidst all the tragedy, this was comforting.

The court recessed for the weekend and began hearing more the following week when

Birmingham introduced forensic evidence. This was given by Dr Bríd McBride, one of the forensic experts who had found blood spattering at the flat in Richmond Cottages. This information was required to support the version of events outlined in the defendant's statements, which claimed Noor had died in Richmond Cottages. It was tactical evidence.

Marie Mulhall took the stand on Tuesday, 17 October. She had watched the trial unfold from the public gallery. Occasionally, in the recesses, she had come down to embrace and talk to Charlotte. She would hold her arm and hug her, telling her everything would be fine.

After she was sworn in, Marie was asked to recount the confession that Charlotte had made to her just days after the killing.

She spoke honestly and sincerely, and never deviated from what she had told the gardaí in her statement. Everyone present in the court, without exception, appreciated the difficult position she was in. Yet the various spectators couldn't help but admire her honesty, and desire to do the right thing in the face of such adversity.

She recounted what Charlotte had told her; primarily that Noor had tried to rape her sister Linda.

'Charlotte was very upset. I'd just come in from work and she came to my room crying. I asked what was wrong with her. She appeared to be drunk. She told me she was upset because they were after killing Farah.'

Asked by Birmingham what her immediate reaction to this was, she said: 'I didn't believe it. She told me it was herself and Linda. She didn't say too much about my mother but I knew my mother had been there. I just let her tell me what she was saying.

'Charlotte and she had been in the chipper and they came in the apartment where they found Farah trying to rape my sister Linda. Charlotte tried to get Farah off and he turned on her.'

Birmingham then asked if she continued to disbelieve her sister's story. In response, she said: 'I didn't believe her at all until I heard it on the radio that a body had been taken from the canal.'

Isobel Kennedy, the senior counsel representing Charlotte, conducted a short cross-examination. She asked about her statement, which suggested the conversation had been in the bathroom of the house and not in the bedroom.

Marie didn't deviate: 'That could be a misprint. I know the conversation took place in my bedroom.'

Kennedy put it to her that her client had never said a word, causing her to reply: 'I disagree with that.'

*****

It was noteworthy that the statements furnished to the detective team by Noor's former partner had been disclosed to the defence for legal reasons. The prosecution, predicting the defence would correctly seek to portray Noor as a violent thug, decided to call her as a witness, rather than have the defence do it.

There was a general feeling on all sides that her evidence could heavily influence the jury.

Her testimony was heartbreaking. She spoke of the beatings and rapes she suffered at Noor's hands. This evidence had a clear effect on the jury, who were left in no doubt about the true nature of Noor's personality.

Perhaps the most important evidence given in the trial came from Mangan and Gerry McDonnell, the detective to whom Charlotte had given her confession. These were among the last to give evidence. Their testimony, which involved reading the various statements into the record, was crucial to both sides.

The defence for both Linda and Charlotte had decided against allowing the sisters to take the stand. It was the general consensus that it would be best if the detectives explained the emotional impact the killing had on their clients.

There is no doubt that this decision was the correct one as it introduced impartiality to the trial. The lawyers hoped the jury might pity the sisters on hearing about the calamitous affect the killing had on them.

When Mangan stepped into the witness box, he was asked recall the confessions Linda had made to him back in August 2005. The detective inspector spoke as openly and honestly as he could.

He took Birmingham through the confessions and Linda's admissions. But there is no doubt that he made a point of emphasising that she had continually wept, often with tears streaming down her face, while she confessed.

'I knew it was an emotional time for her but she indicated she wanted to talk to us. She couldn't get the thoughts of it out of her mind,' he stated.

Linda sat with her head bowed as her own statement was read aloud to the jury. She partly covered her face with her long blonde hair, and occasionally sobbed. At one stage, she asked for a break. She was feeling faint and ready to collapse. This was granted by the trial judge.

Grehan conducted a brief cross examination of Mangan to try reinforcing the sincerity of Linda's regret over what had happened. Mangan spoke with honesty when he said the gardaí had been making limited progress in the case until she had contacted them. He didn't let the matter rest there. He went further, saying the killing had a traumatic effect on Linda. This was the truth. He also mentioned that she had turned to alcohol, and had slashed her arms.

He then went on to reveal how her father John had taken his own life just before Christmas, whilst her mother had disappeared. When he stepped out of the box, Linda looked at him momentarily; there was nothing more he could do.

Detective Sergeant Gerry McDonnell made another compelling witness. He spoke about Charlotte, whom he had interviewed. When he took the stand, he told Birmingham that Charlotte had confessed on 17 October. The statement she made was also read out to the jury.

McDonnell told how she initially denied she had been at the flat at the time of the killing.

He recounted how she claimed to have found her mother, Kathleen, covered in blood. He too spoke about how Charlotte had cried, and agreed she loved her sister, and had wanted to protect her. And like Mangan, he spoke freely and without hesitation about Noor's violence towards women, adding that Kathleen had also made allegations of assault against Noor.

The trial lasted ten days in total. In her closing speech for the prosecution, Úna Ní Raifeartaigh told the jury that some of the evidence they heard had been distressing, disturbing and shocking.

She urged the jury to carefully decide what to make of the evidence, and said the prosecution would be inviting them to come to the conclusion that this was a case of murder. However, she told the jury members they must also consider the defence of provocation, and self-defence in relation to both of the accused.

Grehan spoke eloquently for Linda. He wanted the jury to consider the cases against the sisters separately. This was crucial from his point of view.

He pointed out the simple facts of the case. He said his client had been frightened, and there was a clear indication of a sexual motive on the part of Noor when she said he grabbed her.

Speaking without fear of contradiction, he proclaimed the prosecution had also failed to prove that Linda had caused the death of Noor. He pointed out that Noor's head had never been recovered, and the only evidence of the cause of death was in fact injuries to the torso.

In his summation, it was entirely possible that Noor had already been fatally injured. He pointed out that it was open to the jury to bring in a verdict of 'accessory after the fact' of the killing.

In her closing speech, Isobel Kennedy also invited the jury to conclude that Charlotte had initially denied involvement in the killing in order to protect her sister, the one person she was 'utterly devoted to.' This was true.

She too urged the jury to consider all the facts. She said a finding of self-defence could be used in relation to oneself, but also to another person. The defence of provocation, she argued, could also reduce the offence of murder to manslaughter where there was a total loss of self-control due to the words and actions of the victim.

Linda and Charlotte never flinched; instead they remained impassive as their lawyers spoke on their behalf. In truth, they both knew there was nothing they could say or do. They were in the hands of the jury.

Before the jury rose to consider its verdict, Judge Carney spoke. He told them there could be four verdicts open to them in respect of each accused. He said they could be found guilty of murder, or in the case of provocation, that offence could be reduced to manslaughter.

He urged the jury to consider whether either woman had acted in self-defence, which could reduce murder to manslaughter, or in fact, result in a complete acquittal. When he finished speaking, the jury were led away to debate the evidence. Judge Carney then rose and returned to his chambers. It was up to the jury to decide their fate.

Chapter Ten

'Conscience is the chamber of justice.'

- Origen, early Christian writer

ALONE IN THE court, Charlotte and Linda knew they were in the hands of a jury who would decide their fate.

There was nothing more that anyone could do. Privately, they must have realised they would be found guilty of some crime; now everything depended on the conviction, and the sentence the judge would impose.

Noor's death—even before they had been charged—had a powerful effect on the country. There was no escaping the media interest in the trial, nor the two accused. Ever since they had been charged, they had not had a minute's peace. The tabloids had even given them nicknames: they were called the 'Scissor Sisters'. In truth, they blocked as much of this hyperbole from their minds as possible. Uncertain about how to react or respond, they became more inward looking; never before had they been so alone.

They exchanged secret glances, went outside to smoke cigarettes, and sometimes, when the guards would allow them, spoke to their immediate family who came to support them. It seemed clear to themselves, and everyone familiar with the trial, that the evidence was stacked against them.

To the impartial observer, it was simply a matter of deciding whether the jury would return a verdict of murder, or possibly manslaughter. Still, there was always hope.

The seasoned court observers were of the opinion that the jury would return within an hour to deliver a verdict. This assumption, in time, like everything else to do with the killing of Farah Swaleh Noor, would prove to be nothing more than idle thinking.

In contrast to what they expected, when the jury returned to the courtroom a few hours into their deliberations; Judge Carney told them he would accept a majority verdict, in which at least

10 jurors formed the majority. However, he was unequivocal in his desire for a unanimous verdict.

Then a forewoman stood up and explained that they had not yet reached any verdict; this was an unexpected development which took many by surprise. Judge Carney decided to send them to a hotel for the night, where they could rest, and begin their deliberations once more the following morning.

In contrast to what everyone expected, it appeared that the jury were finding it difficult to come to a decision. This had to be interpreted as a good sign.

The next day, at 11am, they returned to the courtroom. Judge Carney sent them away to deliberate the intricacies of the trial once again. Time passed slowly for the two sisters, who despite the trauma that engulfed them, were looking healthy.

The jury emerged at lunchtime, but there was no news. It was at this point that a gradual fear began to grow among onlookers in the court. Although no one dared mention it; there was a possibility that the sisters could be acquitted.

The atmosphere lent itself to coincidences. Still there was no news, even after the jury returned from lunch, and once again resumed their deliberations.

Later that same evening, the courtroom was engulfed with the rumour and counter-rumour of a hung jury. Mangan began to look concerned. Members of the detective team stood around the round hall in small groups, chatting amongst themselves and wondering aloud; this made no sense to any of them.

Hours later, they were called back into the court in time for the jury to emerge from the deliberations room. The defence and prosecution teams quickly assembled themselves in time for the court clerk to announce Judge Carney's entrance with the words, 'All rise.'

When the judge had taken his seat, the forewoman stood up and said that they still had not made up their minds.

Most people agreed that they were having difficulty in deciding a verdict. The interpretation of this was to the benefit of the two accused, especially Linda, who had wept openly when her statement was read to the court. This had, in the opinion of some, disturbed the jury and caused them to see her as a vulnerable woman rather than a ruthless killer. There was no doubting that something was causing them to think before coming to a decision.

Aware of the rights of the accused, Judge Carney urged them once more to continue with their deliberations in the morning, and sent them to a hotel once again.

The failure of the jury to return a quick verdict caused a degree of confusion among the media, who had broadly speculated that Charlotte and Linda would be convicted, but even with this rationale, could not understand what was taking so long.

*****

The next morning, the jury returned once again at 11am and vanished into their deliberations room once Judge Carney had officially opened a new court session. After hours of secret deliberations, they appeared again.

This time, the jury forewoman told Judge Carney that they were deadlocked. Her words sent shockwaves through the courtroom. Though all eyes were on the jury, Charlotte and Linda looked more than taken aback. The jury had deliberated for more than 14 hours at this stage. Without intending to, the jury had thrown Linda and Charlotte a lifeline. The sisters looked at the forewoman, trying to read her eyes, but they could not detect the slightest clue as to what was happening.

It was now Friday night. Mangan could not believe the jury hadn't delivered a verdict, leading to speculation of an acquittal. In such a situation, Mangan would have preferred a re-trial. Judge Carney remained impassive. He was still of the opinion that justice should prevail no matter what, and encouraged the jury to continue discussing the matter.

In doing so he said: 'There are five children who have a vital interest in this, as you know, and we're anxious to reach a conclusion.

'If you're in any doubt as to the evidence, you should resolve it in favour of the accused, and if there's any further help I can give you I'll be delighted to do so.'

He was of course referring to Linda's four children and Charlotte's baby boy. However, the remark caught the prosecution team by surprise. Birmingham rose to his feet as soon as the jury had vanished into their private room. He objected to the Judge's comment.

Judge Carney, speaking with absolute con-viction, stood up and said aloud; 'Get real Mr Birmingham,' before disappearing into his chambers. The exchange added more drama to the courtroom.

Later that evening, the jury emerged once more and took their seats. Minutes later, Judge Carney returned to his seat. This time, the jury forewoman stood up, and speaking with as much authority as she could muster, told the judge that they had come to a deadlock, only to have Judge Carney urge them to deliberate for a further half-hour.

However, shortly afterwards they returned. They requested that they go to a hotel for a third night. The forewoman said: 'We're talked out. The air upstairs is blue and we wish to come back to this tomorrow.'

This was interpreted as a good sign. What Linda and Charlotte made of the legal jousting will never be known. The sisters looked relaxed. Linda, more than Charlotte, had settled into the routine of the trial and no longer found it intimidating. In the last days of the hearings, they had arrived to the court neatly dressed. Linda wore a shirt and a leather jacket, though she kept the piercing above her upper lip.

Charlotte, who had just had a baby, made a similar impression, but she dressed in denim. Though she wore her hair in a pony tail, it was her eyes that attracted the most attention. Like Linda, she wore heavy eye-liner, which overstated her features. This, perhaps more than anything else, was a mask that detracted attention away from the stomach

-churning anguish that overcame her every time she thought about losing her baby. Although the courtroom was besieged with reporters, none saw the panic on the accused sisters' faces because they masked it so well.

The next day, at 11am sharp, the trial resumed in the Central Criminal Court. The jury were now escorted everywhere by a team of gardaí assigned to protect them and keep them from discussing the trial with anyone outside the jury. That morning was a Saturday, hence the Four Courts complex was empty, but it had been specially opened for the trial.

A scattering of journalists hovered around the round hall outside Court No. 2, waiting in anticipation. Once again, when the jury arrived and appeared before Judge Carney, they vanished from sight into their private room. They emerged an hour later, prompting excitement, but they only wanted to have a cigarette break.

Then, an hour later, rumours circulated that they had come to a decision. It had been three days and the jury had deliberated for 18 hours and one minute exactly.

There was total silence in the court as the jury took their seats. Their entrance was followed by Judge Carney, who returned to the hushed courtroom, and took his seat. Then the forewoman stood up and announced that they had reached a decision. Linda and Charlotte held hands and didn't say a word.

The forewoman passed a note to the court clerk, who asked if they had reached a decision. The answer was yes.

Linda had been found guilty of manslaughter; Charlotte guilty of murder.

The facts were as follows: 11 members of the panel agreed that Linda was guilty of manslaughter, while 10 convicted Charlotte of the murder of the Kenyan.

Judge Carney then thanked the jury for its careful attention to the verdict, which he said had been a 'discriminatory' one. It was over.

*****

When the verdicts were read out, the sisters did not touch or look at each other. In the silence, both looked down and showed no surprise; their body language never gave them away.

Instead, Charlotte called her solicitor to ask to be allowed to keep her baby. She was distraught; few people thought for a moment about the effects her conviction would have on her little boy.

Isobel Kennedy raised the matter immediately, as her sentence was a forgone conclusion; she would get life imprisonment.

Mangan was seated across the court and looked relieved that it was over, as did the rest of the team.

Moments after the verdicts were delivered, he was called back to the witness box to give evidence. This would assist Judge Carney in imposing a sentence. He had just one opportunity to try to explain his knowledge of the two convicted women.

He began with the facts. Linda, he said, was unemployed and a mother of four young children. Reading from his notes, he said she had a previous conviction for larceny dating back to 1993.

This time, he made a point of emphasising that she came from a troubled background, though the words he used were a 'very tough family background.' He continued, in his own measured way, to recount the horrific life Linda had led. He said there was a history of abuse by a violent partner, who had received a 'substantial jail term' for cruelty to her children.

Next he spoke about Charlotte, who could only think of her baby boy. He said she had a conviction under the Criminal Damage Act and for a public order offence, but she had received probation. He drew attention to the fact that she had a serious problem with drugs and alcohol, and like Linda, came from a 'troubled background.'

Mangan had never seen the sisters as the monsters they were made out to be; he correctly saw them as products of society—a harsh and brutal society.

He referred to the death of their late father John, saying: 'John Mulhall (Snr) was probably in my view the mainstay of the family.'

The court fell silent as he said it was his opinion that the current case had contributed to his death.

*****

There had been no winners in this trial. The jailing of the Mulhall sisters wasn't in itself punishment; separation from their children is what hurt them the most. Though Linda's conviction for manslaughter was a success by all accounts for her legal team; there was no denying this.

Charlotte had been found guilty of murder; there was now nothing anyone could do or say to change that. It was now time for the formalities. Judge Carney next asked about the possibility of a victim impact statement before he sentenced the sisters. Birmingham told him the team had not received any 'great assistance from the Kenyan authorities.'

Judge Carney adjourned sentencing until 4 December, when he would have more information. The court rose once more.

When he left, Charlotte and Linda came back to life. Charlotte hugged her two brothers as she was led down to the cells. Linda now began to cry. 'Thank God it's over,' she said.

She then kissed each of them, and hugged them tightly, touching their faces, before making her way out of Court No. 2 to join her sister.

She had seemed truly moved by Mangan's evidence, which was delivered in a sincere and truthful way. Before she left, she shook his hand, and thanked him for everything he had done. She also thanked the other members of the team. Few inside the courtroom fully understood how she had been haunted by Noor's killing, though Mangan knew full well.

*****

Linda and Charlotte Mulhall had always accepted they would end up in prison when they began the arduous task of confessing. Linda had been the first to tell the truth. Charlotte had only confessed when confronted with Linda's admission. In this regard, their incarceration had never been in doubt. Once Linda had made the decision to reveal the truth; her future had been decided. Perhaps, she saw this as a way of absolving herself of the guilt that consumed her.

She had stood to gain nothing by confessing to Mangan; she had not sought a deal, or even attempted to secure a lesser sentence. Instead she had told the truth and done what was asked of her.

It was noteworthy that she had never attempted to blame anyone else for the killing; on the contrary, she had placed her own liberty at risk to protect her father. Of course, she had lied in the beginning, but when she made the mental decision to tell the truth, she did so with a degree of honestly that is a rare occurrence.

Charlotte's sentence had been a forgone conclusion. Because she had been convicted for murder, her lawyers knew she had to receive a mandatory life sentence. Linda's case was starkly different; the jury had convicted her for manslaughter, which afforded her trial judge an opportunity to impose a lesser sentence.

Most people agreed that this was likely to happen, but even with this rationale, they knew she would end up in prison for a long time. The sisters returned to Court No. 2 for sentencing on 4 December.

That morning, Judge Carney heard the defence and prosecution make submissions to have the sentencing of the sisters adjourned. The prosecution said the detective team were making efforts to bring the victim's mother to Ireland to provide a victim impact report.

In their applications, the defence had argued that psychiatric and probation reports were still not ready; they too wished to have the sentencing adjourned. However, Judge Carney rejected the applications on the grounds that both sides had 'ample time' to prepare.

This was an unexpected development, particularly for Brendan Grehan, the senior counsel, who had represented Linda. He had been retained to represent Pádraig Nally, a farmer who had shot a traveller at his farm in Co. Mayo. That trial had begun hearing evidence in another court across the round hall.

Therefore when Judge Carney took his seat in Court No. 2, and moved to begin the sentencing hearing, it soon became apparent that Grehan was missing. Judge Carney then asked where Grehan's junior counsel was. The judge didn't adjourn the case but sat motionless, then pronounced: 'Well, we will just have to wait until one of them appears,' he declared.

Their absence had been an unfortunate error and was not deliberate. Grehan had told his junior that he would represent Linda at her sentencing, but unfortunately had been delayed because he was involved in another important trial. This was beyond anyone's control. The court sat in silence for ten minutes while efforts were made to locate the barristers. Minutes later, Grehan hurried in, offered his apologies, and prepared to make a submission for leniency on behalf of his client, Linda. The hearing then proceeded.

Grehan, who had managed to achieve a result by having Linda's charge reduced to manslaughter, now pleaded with the judge to show mitigation. In spite of everything, he said she had co-operated with the investigation, had been remorseful and was the mother of four children. The barrister went further. He said Linda was a 'good mother to those children.'

This prompted Judge Carney to intervene at once. He referred to the time when Linda had said she 'wanted to make a trifle for the children rather than go out with gardaí.'

As far as he was concerned, he said he could not accept that someone who put herself in this situation was a good mother.

In a slow and methodical manner, the judge explained what he was about to do. He began by saying the case had been 'the most grotesque case of killing that has occurred within my professional lifetime. So as far as Charlotte is concerned, the sentence is a mandatory one of imprisonment for life.'

Whilst it was open to him to impose a life sentence for manslaughter, he said the jury had allowed the defence of provocation, and he should respect that. What he said next dimmed the hopes of any reprieve as far as Linda was concerned.

He started off by saying that there were many factors in Linda's dysfunctional background that the jury had already taken into account in determining the defence of provocation. He noted that she had been highly co-operative with the gardaí. He said she had been 'very frank in her admissions.'

He went to a great deal of trouble to explain his rationale before he delivered his sentence. In a review of 50 cases of manslaughter, which had been originally tried as murder cases, he said 14 years had been the longest term imposed.

There would be no mitigation for Linda on the grounds of her dysfunctional life. This, he said, permitted him to sentence her to 15 years, but he repeated that if she was, 'a good mother, she would not have been getting herself into a situation of this kind.'

The drama didn't end there.

When she heard the sentence; Linda held her face in her hands, and began to cry. This was the moment she had dreaded. In truth, she was devastated and inconsolable. She was troubled by the idea that she would never get to see her children growing up. There were no encouraging signs.

Perhaps she asked herself if she and Charlotte had done the right thing by confessing. Their lives were now ruined for ever. The nightmare had ended, but in many ways it had just begun.

Her father had committed suicide and her children would be without a mother. No matter what way she examined the situation, she was the loser. And to the forefront of her mind was the undeniable fact that her own mother was nowhere to be seen.

EPILOGUE

THE DAY OF the sentencing had been a calamitous one for Linda and her sister Charlotte. The younger of the two had accepted her fate after she was found guilty of the murder; Charlotte knew she would waste away her young life in jail when found guilty; there was nothing that anyone could do to change this destiny.

Linda, though, had privately hoped for a miracle. Her prayers had partially been answered when she was found guilty of manslaughter and not murder, but the nightmare she had found herself trapped in returned to consume her when she was sentenced to 15 years.

No matter what way she rationalised her predicament; she could not help but come to the conclusion that she had no future. She has already appealed the severity of her sentence in the beleaguered hope that a higher court will review her case. In the meantime, she has accepted the sentence handed down because she has no other choice.

In truth, Linda and Charlotte Mulhall never really had any choices in life. Drugs, alcohol, and low self-esteem dictated the course of their lives ever since they were young girls. Are they ruthless killers? Most likely not. They are best described as vulnerable women who, while high on drugs and alcohol, carried out unspeakable acts on their victim. They now hold the reputation of being notorious killers, with their own nickname, the 'Scissor Sisters'.

Though, having become one the biggest stories in recent criminal history; they have gotten on with their lives as best they can. Their worlds have changed.

Linda and Charlotte now spend their days in the Women's Prison in Mountjoy, where they live in cells next to each other. Perhaps this has been some sort of consolation.

Charlotte has since appeared before the courts fuelling further interest in her. She was convicted for failing to turn up to face charges of prostitution. She is doing her best to care for her baby boy, who is brought to visit her in the Dóchas centre in the prison every week.

Linda, though, is still trying to come to terms with being separated from her children. Her devotion to them—though not always the best— was always proverbial. She is occasionally allowed to see them; those who know her best say she is just about coping with life without them.

She has only made one public comment about her case. And that was to say she had never been involved in prostitution—an untrue allegation that has circulated about her. She won't talk about the killing; those who know her say she still can't cope with it.

She and Charlotte were recently visited by Mangan, who asked if they would provide more evidence against their mother Kathleen, whom the Garda are actively seeking. Charlotte said she couldn't help. Initially, Linda agreed to co-operate but then changed her mind; she had had enough.

It was time to put the killing and dismember-ment of Farah Swaleh Noor behind her. She wants to get on with her life.

She says she dreams of opening a beauty salon with Charlotte when they are released. She has spoken of this to her friends; in fact, the two women hope to spend their time in prison learning about beauty treatments and business.

They have discovered in themselves a new-found curiosity about learning, which sums up the tragedy of it all. Charlotte has thrown herself into studies: she does little else.

Those who could have helped her and Linda in years gone by, when they were most at risk from drugs and drink, had no desire to.

Circumstances had dictated their fate, and what would become of them. As Linda herself would say, she was always in the wrong place at the wrong time.

So was Farah Swaleh Noor.

There are no winners in this case. A man's life was taken, and his remains denigrated in the most horrific fashion. His children will grow up with stories of how their violent father was himself violently killed and dismembered. Any chance of redemption he may have had was taken away from him.

Charlotte and Linda broke ranks with all social taboos when they tore and cut Noor's body apart. This is compounded by the fact that his head and penis have not yet been recovered. Behind his violent life and legacy, a family also lost a son and several children lost a father. Five other children will be raised without their mothers.

The horrific events described in this book took place over one drug-fuelled night, but the consequences are destined to last for generations.

Glossary

The Mulhalls and Farah Swaleh Noor

Mulhall, Charlotte 'Charlie', sister of Linda.

Mulhall, John, Snr, father of Linda and Charlotte.

Mulhall, Kathleen, mother of Linda and Charlotte.

Mulhall, Linda, sister of Charlotte.

Noor, Farah Swaleh, aka **Sheilila Salim,** killed and dismembered by Linda and Charlotte Mulhall. His remains were discovered in the Royal Canal.

***

An Garda Síochána

Breathnach, Garda Brian and Ferriter, Garda Eoin took the first remains from the canal water.

Bruton, Sergeant John, of the Garda Sub-Aqua Unit.

Cox, Detective Garda Dominic, filmed Linda as she retraced her steps from the night of the killing.

Crime and Security, the spying department of Garda headquarters.

Crimestoppers, organisation seeking information on crime from the general public.

Criminal Law Act, 1997, under which Linda, Charlotte, John and Kathleen Mulhall were first arrested.

Dunne, **Detective Malachy,** and **Detective Patrick Flood**, interviewed Bakaar and Hyland.

Fitzgibbon Street Garda Station, the nearest station to the scene of the discovery.

Garda Control, Harcourt Square.

Garda Sub-Aqua Unit, the specialist team tasked with recovering the remains from the Royal Canal.

Garda Technical Bureau, offering forensic analysis and examination.

Greally, Garda Alan took the call from Tara Street and entered the incident on the Grada PULSE information system.

Hickey, Detective Sergeant Liam, who first arrested Charlotte Mulhall.

Interpol, the international police agency who ran checks in an attempt to identify the remains.

Keegan, Detective Garda Patrick, interviewed Kathleen Mulhall.

Kenna, Detective Dan, compiled the statements into a book of evidence.

Kilmainham Garda Station, where John Mulhall was brought for questioning.

Labuschagne, Superintendent Gerard, of the Ritual Killing Unit of the South African Police Force in Pretoria, consulted regarding the possibility of a ritual killing.

Leahy, Garda Mick, Duty Sergeant the night Linda Mulhall made her recorded statement at Tallaght Garda Station.

Mangan, Detective Inspector Christy, in charge of the overall investigation.

McDonnell, Detective Sergeant Gerry, experienced detective from Fitzgibbon Street who first arrested Kathleen Mulhall.

McKeown, Detective Superintendent John, the overall head of the investigation.

Mountjoy Garda Station, where Charlotte was taken for her interrogation.

Mountjoy Women's Prison, Phibsboro, where Linda and Charlotte were sentenced to imprisonment.

National Bureau of Criminal Investigation, the state agency for major crime investigation.

O'Brien, **Detective David,** who first arrested John Mulhall.

O'Connell, Detective Sergeant Walter, first arrested Linda Mulhall.

PULSE, Garda computer system.

Ramsbottom, Dr Dorothy, of the Forensic Science Laboratory, confirmed a DNA match between Noor, the crime scene and Noor's son from a previous relationship.

Roche, Sergeant Shay, formally charged Linda.

Store Street Garda Station, a central Garda station in Dublin city.

Tallaght Garda Station, the nearest such station to Kilclare Gardens.

***

The Fire Brigade

Carroll, **Derek,** district fire officer.

Cullen, **Andrew,** fireman.

Mannelly, **Glen,** a fireman in Tara Street.

Phibsboro Fire Station, near the Royal Canal.

Tara Street Fire Station, a command and control unit in Dublin city centre.

***

Forensics

Auguestin, Dr, an Isotope Analysis expert in Belfast.

Curtis, **Dr Michael,** Deputy State Pathologist.

Dublin City Morgue, where the post-mortem of Noor was carried out.

Fakih, Dr Y.M. called to the scene to confirm the remains were human and pronounce death officially.

Isotope Analysis, a process whereby the likely

nationality of a body can be determined through the examination of the diet, through the intestines, and oxygen.

McBride, Dr Bríd, a forensic scientist.

***

Locations

Brittas, an area near Tallaght Linda walked to with Noor's head.

Clarke's Bridge, the specific location on the Royal Canal where Charlotte and Linda chose to dump the remains of Noor.

Gardiner Street, in Dublin's north inner city.

Kilclare Gardens, Fettercairn, Tallaght, at the foot of the Dublin Mountains.

Killinarden Park, and **Killinarden Hill,** green areas near Tallaght.

Lamh District, the Coast Province, Kenya, where Noor was born.

Liffey boardwalk

Lismore House, Drumcondra, where Kathleen stayed after leaving Mountainview.

Mombassa, where Noor's mother lives.

O'Connell Street, Dublin's main thoroughfare.

17 Richmond Cottages, in Dublin's north inner city area of Ballybough, where the killing of Noor occurred.

Royal Canal, the waterway running through Ballybough.

Sean Walsh Memorial Park, a park near the Square.

Terenure College, where John Mulhall was first arrested.

Square Shopping Centre, Tallaght, The

Summerhill Parade, a thoroughfare in the north inner city of Dublin where Kathleen was first arrested.

Sunset House Pub, a bar in the north inner city.

Tymon Park North, a park in Tallaght near the Square.

***

Witnesses

Abdulaziz, Ali Suleiman, a friend of Noor, who Kathleen asked about Noor after he had been killed.

Andrews, Mary, the manager at the Mountainview.

Bob, Hanji and Catalin, who ran Lismore House.

Burke, Caitriona, the new tenant at No. 1, 17 Richmond Cottages, who gave gardaí permission to run forensic tests in her home.

Farrelly, Dermot, a community Welfare Officer who was told by Kathleen that Noor had left her and asked about his whereabouts.

Gannon, Margaret, a witness who saw the body parts in the canal.

Kearney, Paul, a witness who saw the body parts in the canal.

Keegan, Laurence, a retired army private who saw the half-buried head of Noor in Sean Walsh Memorial Park.

Mohamed, Ibrahim, a friend of Noor, who was told

by Kathleen that he had left her.

Noor, Mohammed Ali, a friend of Noor, who contacted another friend, **Rashid Omar Ahmed,** asking him to enquire about Noor's whereabouts through contacts in Dublin and Cork.

O'Connor, Derek, of the Asylum Seekers Unit.

O'Connor, James, a witness who saw the body parts in the canal and phoned 999.

Said, Husna Mohamed, Noor's wife in Kenya.

Shigoo, Somoe Bakari, Noor's mother in Kenya.

Steinle, Peter, a witness who saw the body parts in the canal from North Strand Road and phoned Crimestoppers.

Tobin, John, who collected rent from Kathleen Mulhall and was told that Noor had left her.

***

Legal Personnel

Birmingham, George, a barrister who was senior counsel for the state.

Carney, Mr Justice Paul, the presiding judge at the trial of Linda and Charlotte Mulhall.

Gibbons, Judge Conal, Charlotte appeared before him after admitting to her involvement in the killing.

Grehan, Brendan, SC, Linda's representative in court.

Kennedy, Isobel, SC, Charlotte's representative in court, and **Sean Gillane**, who worked alongside her.

Lonergan, John, the Governor of Mountjoy Prison.

Malone, Judge Miriam, Linda appeared before her for the hearing.

McCaffery, Dr Brian, a psychiatrist who stated after examination that Linda Mulhall was unfit, in his opinion, to go to trial.

Ní Raifeartaigh, Una, prosecutor.

O'Doherty, John, Charlotte's solicitor

O'Donnell, Judge Hugh, issued the arrest warrant for Linda Mulhall.

Sheehan, Robert, from the prosecutor's office.

Tunney, Kevin, a Tallaght solicitor who specialises in criminal law.

***

Other Notes

'Adam' Investigation, The, a case investigated by the Metropolitan Police in London after the body of an unknown young male was found in the Thames. He was believed to have been a victim of muti Killing.

Adecco Recruitment Agency, the job agency through which Noor got his job with Schmitt ECS.

Bestia, Adrian, a young Romanian man found dead in a suitcase in the Royal Canal in July 2001, not far from the site where the torso of Noor was found.

Kafan, a white sheet that is wrapped around a body in preparation for a Muslim burial.

Mecca, where Muhammad, the founder of Islam, was born. People of the Muslim faith must face in the direction of Mecca when they pray

Metro, The, newspaper.

Mohangi, Shan, a medical student who killed and dismembered his 16-year-old girlfriend in Dublin in

1963.

Murray, Raonaid, a teenage girl stabbed to death near her home in Dun Laoghaire in 1999. Noor alluded to the fact that he had killed her.

Muti killing, a ritual murder in which the vital organs of the victim are harvested while they are still alive, used in some cultures with the belief that the one carrying out the ritual will gain increased sexual or mental prowess.

Onyemaechi, Paiche, a mother of two and daughter of the Chief Justice of Malawi, Leonard Unyolo, whose headless body was found near Piltown, Co. Kilkenny in July 2004.

salat-l-janazah, the Muslim funeral prayer.

Schmitt ECS, the company for whom Noor worked.

Staffords Funeral Home, where the funeral prayers took place.

Street Journal, The newspaper.

Imam, the leader in the Muslim prayers.

THE LAST EXECUTIONER
Memoirs of Thailand's last Prison Executioner

By Chavoret Jaruboon
with Nicola Pierce

Chavoret Jaruboon was personally responsible for executing 55 prison inmates on Thailand's infamous death row.

As a boy, he wanted to be a teacher like his father, then a rock'n'roll star like Elvis, but his life changed when he joined Thailand's prison service. From there he took on one of the hardest jobs in the world.

Honest and often disturbing—but told with surprising humour and emotion—*The Last Executioner* is the remarkable story of one man's experiences with life and death.

Emotional and at times confronting, the book grapples with the controversial topic of the death sentence and makes no easy reading.

This book is not for the faint hearted—*The Last Executioner* takes you right behind the bars of the Bangkok Hilton and into death row.

To order this book go to www.maverickhouse.com

LOOT
Inside the World of Stolen Art

By Thomas McShane
with Dary Matera

Thomas McShane is one of the world's foremost authorities on the art theft business and in *Loot* he recounts some of his most thrilling cases as he matched wits with Mafia mobsters and smooth criminals.

Covering his 36 years as an FBI Agent, the author brings us on a thrilling ride through the underworld of stolen art and historical artefacts as he donned his many disguises and aliases to chase down $900 million worth of stolen art pieces. In the end, he always got his man, but the way in which he did it each time is told with great energy and imagination.

He worked on high profile cases all over the world, including the Beit heist in Ireland. From Rembrandts robbed in Paris to van Goghs vanishing in New York, McShane's tale is one of great adventure, told with surprising humour.

The Thomas Crown Affair meets *Donnie Brasco* in this story of a truly extraordinary life.

To order this book go to www.maverickhouse.com

FINAL WITNESS
My Journey from the Holocaust to Ireland

By Zoltan Zinn-Collis
with Alicia McAuley

The concentration camp at Bergen-Belsen is the scene of one of the world's largest mass murders. It was here that Zoltan Zinn-Collis was incarcerated as a five year old boy, along with his family and where, incredibly, he managed to survive the inhuman brutality of the SS guards and the ravages of near-starvation, disease and squalor.

Discovered by a Red Cross nurse who pronounced him 'an enchanting scrap of humanity', Zoltan was brought to Ireland and adopted by one of the camp's liberators, Dr Bob Collis. Having endured the physical and mental legacy of his childhood, now, aged 66, Zoltan is ready to speak.

This story is one of deepest pain and greatest joy, told with tremendous honesty and surprising sparks of humour. It is a story of how a young boy lost one family and found another; of how, escaping from the ruins of a broken Europe, he was able to rebuild a new life.

The triumphant story of this remarkable man's journey through the darkness of genocide will inspire anyone whose life has been touched by fear, suffering, and loss.

To order this book go to www.maverickhouse.com

MORE NON-FICTION FROM MAVERICK HOUSE

WELCOME TO HELL
One Man's Fight for Life inside
the 'Bangkok Hilton'

By COLIN MARTIN

Written from his cell and smuggled out page by page, Colin Martin's autobiography chronicles an innocent man's struggle to survive inside one of the world's most dangerous prisons.

After being swindled out of a fortune, Martin was let down by the hopelessly corrupt Thai police. Forced to rely upon his own resources, he tracked down the man who conned him and, drawn into a fight, accidentally stabbed and killed the man's bodyguard.

Martin was arrested, denied a fair trial, convicted of murder and thrown into prison—where he remained for eight years. Honest and often disturbing, Welcome to Hell is the remarkable story of how Martin was denied justice again and again.

In his extraordinary account, he describes the swindle, his arrest and vicious torture by police, the unfair trial, and the eight years of brutality and squalor he was forced to endure.

To order this book go to www.maverickhouse.com